'Many recent accounts of Chile's October 2019 rebellion simplistically trace its origins to a rejection of the legacy of the Pinochet dictatorship's neoliberal economic model. This outstanding volume brings together a collection of stellar scholars to provide a more nuanced account of the origins of the revolt, uncovering the complex interaction between authoritarian legacies, social trauma, and dashed expectations. It is a definitive work for anyone seeking to understand Chile's past, its current political moment and its constitutional path forward'.
– **Peter M. Siavelis,** *Professor of Political Science and International Affairs, Wake Forest University, USA*

'This fine collection proposes a suggestive and persuasive combination of factors for understanding the "social uprising" in Chile from October 2019. Distinguished scholars consider the historical, generational, social, and political dynamics behind a remarkable and unexpected breakdown in the 30-year post-dictatorial consensus. Deep knowledge, open-minded analysis, and the keen desire to review prior understandings of Chilean "modernisation" evident in these chapters will greatly enrich the continuing debate over the qualities of public life and culture in the country'.
– **James Dunkerley,** *Professor of Politics at Queen Mary, University of London, UK*

'Solving the Chilean puzzle of stability and plenty has been something of a mini industry for over a century. The events of October 18th 2019 made contemporary Chile even more of a paradox: thirty years of success followed by a popular demand for drastic change. This book represents our best efforts to understand both the long-term and immediate causes of the explosion and to begin re-imagining a future Chile'.
– **Miguel A. Centeno,** *Musgrave Professor of Sociology, Princeton University, USA*

Social Revolt in Chile

This book investigates why Chile suddenly confronted a violent social revolt in October 2019, after almost thirty years of political stability, during which time the country was broadly regarded as Latin America's most successful nation.

Since democratic restoration in 1990, Chile's relatively high levels of political stability, increasing prosperity and social modernisation have stood out in a region shaken by political convulsion and economic malaise. In early October 2019, President Sebastián Piñera confidently claimed that Chile represented a true 'oasis' of political stability and economic vitality in Latin America. However, just weeks later, the announcement of a small increase in the price of Santiago's underground transport system unleashed an unprecedented wave of violent anti-government protests in the country, with protestors ultimately demanding Piñera's resignation and the end of neoliberalism and the 1980 Constitution, among many other demands. This book analyses the causes of Chile's socio-political upheaval, arguing that the fast social and economic modernisation produced by the neoliberal system led to a series of destabilising socio-political processes in the country.

At a time when much analysis of the October uprising tends to be superficial or polarised on ideological grounds, this book provides a much-needed sociological and institutional analysis of the crisis. It will be an important read for scholars of Latin American politics and development, as well as those with a broader interest in state legitimacy, social movements and political contestation against neoliberalism.

Carlos Peña is Rector of the Universidad Diego Portales and Professor of Law at the Universidad de Chile.

Patricio Silva is Professor of Modern Latin American History at Leiden University, the Netherlands.

Routledge Studies in Latin American Development

The series features innovative and original research on Latin American development from scholars both within and outside of Latin America. It particularly promotes comparative and interdisciplinary research targeted at a global readership.

In terms of theory and method, rather than basing itself on any one orthodoxy, the series draws broadly on the tool kit of the social sciences in general, emphasizing comparison, the analysis of the structure and processes, and the application of qualitative and quantitative methods.

Bolivia at the Crossroads
Politics, Economy, and Environment in a Time of Crisis
Edited by Soledad Valdivia Rivera

Legal Experiments for Development in Latin America
Modernization, Revolution and Social Justice
Helena Alviar García

Brazilian Elites and their Philanthropy
Wealth at the Service of Development
Jessica Sklair

Deepening Democracy in Post-Neoliberal Bolivia and Venezuela
Advances and Setbacks
John Brown

Social Revolt in Chile
Triggering Factors and Possible Outcomes
Edited by Carlos Peña and Patricio Silva

For more information about this series, please visit: www.routledge.com/Routledge-Studies-in-Latin-American-Development/book-series/RSLAD

Social Revolt in Chile
Triggering Factors and Possible Outcomes

**Edited by
Carlos Peña and Patricio Silva**

LONDON AND NEW YORK

First published 2022
by Routledge
2 Park Square, Milton Park, Abingdon, Oxon OX14 4RN

and by Routledge
605 Third Avenue, New York, NY 10158

Routledge is an imprint of the Taylor & Francis Group, an informa business

© 2022 selection and editorial matter, Carlos Peña and Patricio Silva; individual chapters, the contributors

The right of Carlos Peña and Patricio Silva to be identified as the authors of the editorial material, and of the authors for their individual chapters, has been asserted in accordance with sections 77 and 78 of the Copyright, Designs and Patents Act 1988.

All rights reserved. No part of this book may be reprinted or reproduced or utilised in any form or by any electronic, mechanical, or other means, now known or hereafter invented, including photocopying and recording, or in any information storage or retrieval system, without permission in writing from the publishers.

Trademark notice: Product or corporate names may be trademarks or registered trademarks, and are used only for identification and explanation without intent to infringe.

British Library Cataloguing-in-Publication Data
A catalogue record for this book is available from the British Library

Library of Congress Cataloging-in-Publication Data
Names: Peña, Carlos, editor. | Silva, Patricio, editor.
Title: Social revolt in Chile : triggering factors and possible
  outcomes / Carlos Peña, Patricio Silva.
Description: New York : Routledge, 2022. | Includes bibliographical
  references and index.
Subjects: LCSH: Political violence—Chile—History—21st century. |
  Chile—Social conditions—1970– | Social change—Chile—
  History—21st century. | Chile—Economic conditions—1988– |
  Chile—Politics and government—1988– | Government, Resistance—
  Chile-History—21st century. | Protest movements—Chile—
  History—21st century.
Classification: LCC HN300.Z9 V576 2022 (print) | LCC HN300.Z9
  (ebook) | DDC 303.40983—dc23
LC record available at https://lccn.loc.gov/2021046397
LC ebook record available at https://lccn.loc.gov/2021046398

ISBN: 978-1-032-18401-2 (hbk)
ISBN: 978-1-032-18403-6 (pbk)
ISBN: 978-1-003-25435-5 (ebk)

DOI: 10.4324/9781003254355

Typeset in Times New Roman
by Apex CoVantage, LLC

Contents

List of contributors	viii
Acknowledgements	ix
The October revolt in Chile: introduction CARLOS PEÑA AND PATRICIO SILVA	1
1 **Discontent in modernisation: the Chilean case** CARLOS PEÑA	8
2 **The October rebellion: exploring its historical roots** PATRICIO SILVA	28
3 **The rebellion of a disillusioned generation** JOSÉ JOAQUÍN BRUNNER	48
4 **Social policies, uncertainty and social unrest in Chile** ROSSANA CASTIGLIONI	69
5 **The socio-political dynamic of the constituent process** CLAUDIO A. FUENTES	85
Beyond the revolt: the Chile that is coming CARLOS PEÑA AND PATRICIO SILVA	103
Index	112

Contributors

José Joaquín Brunner is Professor at the Centre for Comparative Policies in Higher Education (CPCE) at Universidad Diego Portales, Chile.

Rossana Castiglioni is Professor of Political Science and Dean of the Faculty of Social Sciences and History at Universidad Diego Portales, Chile.

Claudio A. Fuentes is Professor at the Department of Political Science at the Universidad Diego Portales, Chile.

Carlos Peña is Rector of the Universidad Diego Portales and Professor of Law at the Universidad de Chile.

Patricio Silva is Professor of Modern Latin American History at Leiden University, the Netherlands.

Acknowledgements

This book is the result of a collective academic effort. The five scholars involved in this project participated in early 2021 in an online course for post-graduate students from the Universidad Diego Portales in Chile and Leiden University in the Netherlands. The course focused on the socio-economic, political and cultural causes of the social upheaval occurred in Chile from October 18th 2019 onwards. During the lectures, the five scholars engaged with each other and the students in fruitful discussions about the relative importance of each of the mentioned factors which could have helped to originate the revolt. At the end, the idea to translate the results of that fruitful academic dialogue into an edited book emerged as a natural one.

The editors want to thank each of the colleagues who contributed to this book for their enthusiasm and readiness to translate the essence of their presentations into a written piece. Special thanks go to Emma Going for her translation of the contributions from Spanish into the English language. We also would like to express our gratitude to Helena Hurd and Rosie Anderson from Routledge and Rajalakshmi Ramesh for their encouragement and good advice.

The October revolt in Chile
Introduction

Carlos Peña and Patricio Silva

Since democratic restoration in 1990, Chile has been considered globally as one of the most successful countries in Latin America. There are reasons for this. Over the last three decades, Chile has, indeed, been characterised by strong economic growth, a high degree of political stability and a spectacular decrease in poverty. For a long time, Chile has, therefore, been seen by different international bodies as the main candidate for becoming the first developed country in Latin America. The progress Chile has experienced contrasts dramatically with that of the rest of the Latin American region which, over the past few decades, has experienced ongoing political and social upheaval and recurrent economic crises.

If the country is regarded from a broader historical perspective, it is easy to see that Chile has always been an exception in Latin America. Although riots and constitutional changes are not unusual in Latin America – a fertile region for rewriting constitutional texts – Chile has traditionally been an exception among its neighbours in the continent. Effectively, this country managed to consolidate and streamline its state in the first decades of the nineteenth century, long before the rest of the region. In addition, during the nineteenth century, it was able to create a limited but stable democracy that lasted until the second half of the twentieth century, making it one of the oldest in the world. Even Pinochet's dictatorship was an exception in the region. Not only was it one of the most repressive, but it also inspired a modernisation that was different to the simple military *caudillismo* specific to the region. It also distanced itself from simple military corporativism. At the beginning of the twenty-first century – with democracy restored – Chile's exceptionalism seemed to have been consolidated. In barely three decades, the country had achieved a high level of democratic stability thanks to centre-left governments that ended up ruling for twenty-four years. They managed to gradually eliminate many aspects of the dictatorship's legacy. On the other hand, and despite its support to the Pinochet regime in the past, during the Piñera governments, the

DOI: 10.4324/9781003254355-1

Chilean right began to take an increasing distance from the dictator's authoritarian legate. The result of this was an important change in Chilean society's material conditions of existence: poverty went down by more than 50 per cent from its level at the beginning of the 1990s to less than 10 per cent and higher education became universal; intergenerational mobility increased; the middle class expanded to nearly 70 per cent of the population and the country had the highest level of human development in the region. As a result of all this, it seemed to be approaching what international agencies usually call development.

It does not seem out of place, then, that at the beginning of October 2019, Chilean President Sebastián Piñera affirmed with undeniable pride and satisfaction that Chile was a true 'oasis' of political stability and economic vitality in Latin America.

There were reasons to back this up. At the end of August 2019, President Piñera took part in the G7 summit in Biarritz as a special guest of French President Emmanuel Macron. This was a clear demonstration of the international prestige that Chile and the country's economy enjoyed among leaders of the developed world. In addition, Chile was preparing to host two important and prestigious international summits before the end of the year. In mid-November, the APEC (Asia-Pacific Economic Cooperation) Forum was going to be held in Santiago. More than 7,000 delegates were expected from 27 Asian and Latin American countries. Among the leaders who had confirmed their attendance were none other than Vladimir Putin, Donald Trump and Xi Jinping. At the beginning of December 2019, Chile was also going to host the United Nations Climate Change Summit (COP25), with more than 25,000 delegates expected from all over the world. Both summits would have cemented Piñera's position in the international sphere and the possible consolidation of neoliberalism in the country.

Nothing seemed to indicate that Chile was about to suffer the worst sociopolitical crisis the country had experienced since the breakdown of democracy in 1973. Only a few weeks after the president described Chile as an oasis within the region, everything changed. The announcement of a small increase in the price of Santiago underground tickets unleashed an unprecedented wave of violent anti-government protests in Santiago and in other cities throughout the country. Over the weeks, the protests became more and more radicalised, with some observers even considering them completely insurrectionary, politically and culturally speaking. The protesters ended up asking Piñera's resignation, the end of neoliberalism and the derogation of the 1980 Constitution, among a long list of demands. Since then, the streets of Santiago have been filled with all kinds of graffiti, revealing that the cause of the riots goes deeper than a simple protest by users of the underground. This street graffiti shows clear signs of a more heterogeneous protest that has brought together traditionally excluded minorities such as native people, feminists, sexual minorities and generational-cultural identities, as well as demanding class recognition and better pensions and healthcare from older generations. This movement lacked a specific structure or ideological orientation and emerged beyond the party system. Suddenly and spontaneously, it was as if different sectors of society raised a specific grievance and took it out onto the streets.

In a question of hours, these protests became a widespread uprising that was fully supported by left-wing political parties and by a broad range of social movements. At the end of that day, 20 underground stations had been destroyed and another 41 stations were severely damaged. The protests lasted for several months. These demonstrations were often accompanied by violence and the looting of supermarkets, shopping centres, pharmacies and other kinds of shop in the country's city centres. The government responded by using force and deploying riot police and was later forced to declare martial law and mobilise military personnel onto the streets of the main cities. Security forces were clearly overwhelmed by the widespread and violent nature of the protests and, above all, by how long they lasted. After what happened on October 18th and the immediate deterioration of the country's political and security situation, both international summits were cancelled. From October 18th to the beginning of the coronavirus pandemic in Chile in March 2020, Chile was in a state of ongoing socio-political upheaval.

As of today, the majority of Chileans and political analysts are still questioning the main causes of the socio-political unrest that affected the country from October 2019 onwards. The explanation that immediately appeared after the events of October 18th and which soon became popular in the international press was that the main catalyst for the socio-political 'outburst' in Chile was the evident inequalities existing in the country. In addition, other interpretations underlined the responsibility of President Sebastián Piñera, who had created expectations that were too high among the population during the presidential elections that brought him to power for the second time. During the battle for the presidency, Piñera had promised to restore the high levels of economic growth that the country had experienced in the recent past. However, during 2019, it became evident that, although the economy was visibly improving, the rhythm of recovery was much slower than expected. Others saw in the October riots a coordinated political action organised by the Communist Party, anarchist organisations and a series of extreme left groups to force the cancellation of the two international summits in Chile at the end of the year. Both were considered by Chilean left-wing forces as events that would cement Piñera's presence on the international scene and as a test of Chile's full participation in a globalisation process that these sectors openly condemned. Along these same lines, some accused Cuba and Venezuela of being involved in organising the riots of October 18th and the subsequent disturbances. According to this interpretation, they made a concerted effort against Piñera after he led the condemnation in Latin America of Maduro's regime and openly supported the Venezuelan opposition.

Until now, more than a dozen books have been published in Chile about the October 2019 uprising and its possible causes. However, the majority of these publications were written mere weeks or months after what happened that October, in the heat of a tense socio-political situation. Above all, they were written by journalists and political figures who generally adopted a clear political-ideological stance. The majority were written as a sign of support and justification for the uprising, joining the demands for an end to what has been called the 'neoliberal system'.

This book aims to tackle the October uprising and the country's subsequent socioeconomic, political and institutional crisis from a more comprehensive academic perspective. All the contributions in this book use an analytical approach of a sociological and institutional nature. The authors highlight a series of paradoxes that have emerged from the rapid economic modernisation and social transformation the country has experienced in the last forty years. Several of the pieces in this book indicate that, to a certain extent, the neoliberal model in Chile has been a victim of its own success. A common denominator in all of them is their aim of explaining the emergence of the growing 'discomfort' or deep discontent that affects important sectors of Chilean society today. Although all the authors agree that it was the result of countless factors, each of them focuses on a specific one that, in their opinion, was transcendental to the development of the October uprising.

Irrespective of the factors that were decisive to producing the October uprising, it is clear that the protesters who took to the streets identified 'neoliberalism' as the main cause of the country's problems. In fact, the majority of the chants repeated by crowds on the streets and the majority of the slogans on the protesters' placards demanded an end to the neoliberal system in Chile.

This book shows how rapid economic and social development in a country encourages heavily destabilising political processes, particularly when the democratic authorities are not able to adequately channel the lofty expectations of a population that wants to improve its living conditions even more.

In Chapter 1, Carlos Peña evaluates the causes of current social discontent in Chile, concentrating on the dramatic improvement in living and material conditions experienced by Chileans over the last three decades. Since the restoration of democracy in 1990, Chile has successfully modernised and expanded its economy, with its whole population's standard of living and wellbeing becoming the highest in Latin America. This chapter examines three combinations of factors that are perhaps at the root of the current wave of discontent and dissatisfaction affecting an important part of Chilean society. To begin with, it pays attention to the existing relationship between the current disturbances and the radical changes in the material life of millions of Chileans that has led to the so-called paradox of wellbeing. The second combination of factors is related to a series of cultural grievances associated with generational changes. Finally, the chapter also explores the important divisions that have emerged in the political sphere and in key sources of legitimacy, such as the government, Parliament, the legal system and the police. All these examine the context of growing functional differentiation and individuation that occurs in a society undergoing rapid modernisation.

In Chapter 2, Patricio Silva analyses the October 2019 uprising from a long-term historical perspective. The September 1973 coup against Allende and Pinochet's regime (1973–1990) deeply wounded a Chilean society that has still not yet fully healed. The military takeover marked the collapse of Chilean democracy for a long period of time, with years of repression and a radical free market economy following. Pinochet also introduced important legal reforms including the 1980 Constitution. Both neoliberalism and the 1980 Constitution survived to the end of the Pinochet era and have been a permanent source of rebuttal since then by the Chilean left. This chapter analyses the current socio-political unrest in the country from a historical perspective, beginning at the end of the 1960s. The current uprising is considered the cumulation of a long forty-year period in which the Chilean left has constantly struggled against the neoliberal model and the 1980 Constitution introduced by Pinochet. The constant references on the streets to Allende, Pinochet, the Constitution and neoliberalism since the October 2019 uprising are, according to the author, an important reflection of the weight the events of the 1970–1990 period have on the current socio-political Chilean crisis.

In Chapter 3, José Joaquín Brunner focuses on the high expectations created by the expansion of education in the country and the subsequent disillusionment experienced by young people. The Chilean social protests that emerged violently in October 2019 had a distinct sociological identity: they were made up of young people, the participants had a high level of education and women were just as involved as men. This strongly contrasted with the traditional composition of protests in the past, which were dominated by poor urban workers and adult men who generally had a low level of education. The new social composition of the protests reflects the intense economic, social, political and cultural modernisation of Chilean society over the last three decades (1990–2019). This process has given way to a generation, born around 1990, that has played a leading role in the historical expansion of educational opportunities, giving them full secondary school education and then higher education. The author's contention is that, over the last few years, this generation – with its high economic and social expectations – has felt an important sense of frustration. The promise made to integrate this new segment of society into a meritocratic middle-class lifestyle has not been fulfilled. Typical of a disillusioned generation, this dissatisfaction has led to rebellious group behaviour that rejects society's cultural aim of individual success and education as the main vehicle to achieve it.

In Chapter 4, Rossana Castiglioni explores uncertainty and discontent in the new Chilean middle class, which has not enjoyed the fruits of the social policies implemented by the state. Since the transition to democracy in 1990, Chile has been considered a model country in Latin America, with a stable democracy, prosperous economy and notable advances made to reduce poverty. However, in October 2019, the country experienced a sudden social uprising that revealed deep-rooted social discontent. What explains this social uprising? This chapter maintains that reducing poverty brought with it the accompanying expansion of the number of middle-income people facing high levels of uncertainty. These people spend more than they earn, are heavily in debt and their future and opportunities are uncertain. Due to the fact that social security usually has a specific sector in mind and requires proof of resources, they are not eligible for the majority of the benefits of wellbeing, even if they have insufficient income, low-quality jobs and have to pay for costly medical attention. Although they support democracy as a type of regime, they are dissatisfied with its performance, which is why they use protesting to express their discontent. In a context in which politicians and institutions with low levels of legitimacy have, to a great extent, been incapable of tackling the heterogeneous grievances of the middle-income sector of society, the accumulated tension eventually led to a social 'outburst'.

Finally, in Chapter 5, Claudio Fuentes explores how Chile is trying to find an institutional way out of the crisis that abruptly emerged in October 2019. In this chapter, he analyses the attempt to resolve the social and political anxiety created by the 'social uprising' in October 2019 in Chile by beginning a constituent process to change Pinochet's 1980 Constitution. This was one of the main results of a general agreement signed by Parliament at the end of November 2019 in a last-chance attempt to find an institutional way out of the crisis. For many years, surveys have consistently shown that the main concerns and demands of the Chilean population are based on material issues, such as better pensions, education, healthcare and employment. The idea of changing the Constitution was consistently not among people's main concerns. Surprisingly though, in the 2020 referendum, around 80 per cent of the electorate supported the idea of replacing the Constitution through an elected citizen-based Convention. What explains this? This chapter suggests three explanations based on the following factors: the progressive 'constitutionalisation' of citizen demands, the boost these were given by the academic and intellectual community and the specific decisions of the political system that opened up opportunities for a constitutional debate. Therefore, the current constitutional change cannot solely be considered the result of the October uprising. This piece, however, explores the mid-term trends that created the conditions required for replacing the 1980 Constitution introduced by Pinochet.

Many actors have attributed the October uprising to an unresolved desire for constitutional change, something the political and social elite have stubbornly resisted. However, this book intends to make a more careful and detailed analysis of what happened in Chile to show that this was not the case. Social processes are usually the result of multiple factors and, although each event usually has a specific catalyst, this is never the only cause of what occurs. To a European observer, it is probably appealing – although simplistic – to attribute everything that has happened to a rebellion of the Chilean population in order to 'change Pinochet's Constitution' or simply reject the economic model that Chile has built up over the last four decades. Clinging on to this point of view is a blatant oversimplification that any analysis – such as the one in this book – will end up rejecting.

Bringing together the work of some of the most relevant Chilean scholars, this book looks into the causes and factors that may have contributed to the recently described phenomenon. As we will see, each one goes further into helping us understand the phenomenon: the specific discomfort emerging from rapid modernisation, the inheritance of a traumatic political past, the disillusionment of a generation with high expectations as a result of higher education, the high level of debt and uncertainty experienced by the middle classes and the political system crisis and the cleavages that have characterised it are all factors that have conspired to trigger what this book deals with. Of course, none of the authors presume to explain the unknown quantity that is behind this phenomenon, but they do trust that the ideas that spill into their work help make the debate, which will undoubtedly continue to take shape over the next few years, more complex. Encouraging this debate is one of the main aims of this book, which is based on an online course on the October uprising in Chile taught by its authors at the beginning of 2021 to post-graduate students from Leiden University and Diego Portales University.

1 Discontent in modernisation
The Chilean case

Carlos Peña

Introduction

At the end of 2019, one of the most prosperous countries in Latin America, Chile, was getting ready to host both the Asia-Pacific Economic Cooperation summit meeting (APEC) and the United Nations Climate Change conference (COP25), which would bring together almost 30 heads of state. Only two years before, the right had come to power for the second time in a decade, something unprecedented in twentieth century Chilean political history. During these very same days, President Sebastián Piñera described Chile as an oasis in Latin America and a country that was ready to exercise a strong influence over the region.

There are many reasons why the Chilean president described his country like this. On a continent noted for institutional weakness, Chile had enjoyed a long period of democratic stability and a rapid modernisation process. Between 1990 and 2019, its per capita product increased from US$ 4,511 to US$ 25,974 (using international prices; World Bank, 2020), while between 1990 and 2015, the GDP quadrupled in real terms (UNDP, 2017: 361). An official national survey (Casen) showed that poverty had gone down from almost 50 per cent to less than 10 per cent over three decades and from 29.1 per cent to 8.6 per cent between 2006 and 2017 (MDSF, 2019: 14). Between 2002 and 2017, the per capita income of the poorest 10 per cent grew by 145 per cent in real terms (UNDP, 2017: 19). Inequality went down from 054 to 045 according to the Gini Index. Other research shows that if income inequality was measured by group, this had gone down even more. If the data from the Casen surveys between 1992 and 2003 are compared to the data from the ones carried out between 2000 and 2013, the Gini Index falls 26 points (Sapelli, 2016: 48–49). In addition, spending on healthcare and education went up almost three times and consumerism spread, with Chile becoming one of the countries with the highest number of shopping centres in the region. Finally, higher education was opened up to everyone

DOI: 10.4324/9781003254355-2

and became universal (the number of students with this level of education is already about a million) and a broad middle-class sector was created, incorporating more than 60 per cent of the population. All in all – and consistent with this information – another UNDP report placed Chile as one of the countries with a very high level of human development (UNDP, 2019: 344).

What happened almost overnight to turn a country seemingly on the threshold of development into a society with a volatile atmosphere, violence on the streets and permanent discontent? What follows will try to explain this. Of course, it would be an oversimplification to attribute the discontent felt by Chilean society to a single factor, such as inequality or the rejection of a Constitution that was drawn up during a dictatorship that ended thirty years ago. Although these types of argument are frequently put forward in debate to reconstruct events normatively (Dancy, 2000), they tend to be rhetorical and false, inspired by political purposes more than by a desire to understand the phenomenon itself. It would also be an oversimplification to suggest that what occurred in Chile is due to purely idiosyncratic factors and was unconnected to other external events.

The hypothesis that underpins this chapter is that any analysis of what has happened in Chile must consider universal factors associated with modernisation processes as well as unique factors specific to Chile's recent history. As a backdrop, the analysis must bear in mind what is perhaps the most relevant phenomenon in contemporary Chile: the huge and rapid change the country has experienced in terms of the material conditions of its population. This phenomenon – which, in line with the language of social sciences, we could call modernisation, has transformed the country's culture, modified its political cleavage, created a generational distance that has given way to multiple concessions of a cultural nature and left unanswered certain questions that, in dynamic societies, need urgent answers, such as the distribution of the risk of illness and old age. As I will suggest in this chapter, other phenomena that explain discontent, which always seem to accompany these processes and are specific to modern societies, should also be added. Therefore, the causes are varied. A way of approaching these consists of distinguishing between *universality* and *uniqueness*. Historical uniqueness refers to the specific characteristics of a society in a specific time and place; uniqueness alludes to the structural elements that are the basis of this phenomenon. Every society that goes through modernisation processes shares the same basic structural traits. Existence becomes more and more individual, material wellbeing and consumerism increase, the different aspects of social life differ more and more and culture becomes secularised. However, in the light of each society's historical uniqueness, each of these structural aspects acquires specific traits. This distinction can help us understand – at least partly – Chile's situation, where what is universal to modernisation is expressed, making adjustments though for the specific characteristics of its own journey. Distinguishing between both dimensions could help us understand some of the distinctive features of contemporary Chile. This is what we will look at in this chapter.

The universal aspects of discontent

When looking at traditional literature, it is possible to identify a set of phenomena that, like a shadow, accompany modernisation processes and the radical change in the material conditions of existence. This is not, of course, the place to discuss them in detail since that would take our focus away from the case of Chile specifically. However, a general revision of them could help prove that Chilean discontent is not purely an idiosyncratic phenomenon.

As can be seen in the wide range of literature on the topic, modern society is crisscrossed with phenomena that, to a certain point, shape what can be identified as the discomfort that characterises it. Of course, there is a certain rift, a certain cultural duplicity that several authors from George Simmel to Daniel Bell has highlighted (Simmel, 2000: 55ff, 1991; Bell, 1996: 17–41). Modernisation entails the extreme radicalisation and technological advancement of life but, at the same time, also pushes on towards authenticity. The cultural ideal that every human life can self-edit and be true to itself survives. It is as if, in modernity, the Cartesian ideal of a highly rationalised and planned life, on one hand, and the thrust towards spontaneity, on the other, coexist. This rift can be traced back to the early work of authors such as Rousseau and to movements like Romanticism (cf. Starobinski, 1971: 36ff). It is a phenomenon that has been described in literature as having been strongly accentuated in market and monetary economies, which allow for a high level of interaction but a minimal communicational outlay (Luhmann, 2007). Herein lies one of the motives for the indifference within social connections that so damages or irritates new generations. As we will see later on, it is likely that this phenomenon and aspects of it contribute to what we call generational anomie, bestowing on it a touch of cultural struggle that the Chilean protests themselves possess to a great extent. Therefore, what this large body of literature teaches us is that the modern subject's life is, in some way, split and subject to life's extreme radicalisation and the exchange that material wellbeing provides, although they suspect over and over again that the price they pay is too high. Modern individuals live in the middle of this divide, moving between the 'I' they cultivate and the identity they choose, in a world ever more ensnared in the impersonality of a technique that seems to be the only way to obtain the wellbeing they crave.

Together with the split I have just described, the other phenomenon that characterises what is modern is what sociology calls functional differentiation, a trait found in every modernisation process. This involves society losing its centre and breaking up into multiple sub-systems, each with its own specific communicational code. This phenomenon was mentioned early on by Durkheim in his famous paradox about the division of work and was developed in contemporary literature by authors such as Niklas Luhmann (and before him; Parsons, 2021: 137ff). In general terms, this phenomenon consists of life becoming more and more independent at the same time as social connections are slimmed down and get weaker. People need each other more and more but recognise less and less the existence of a world in common. At the end of the nineteenth century, it was easy for society to represent itself as a pyramid with the state at its cusp and political power holding it up and, to a certain extent, modelling it. However, this is no longer possible in modern conditions. Differentiation makes sub-systems autonomous and, when they lose their centre, they become unmanageable for the purposeful government (Luhmann, 1990: 122ff, 2007: 589ff). Needless to say, this is what occurs in the globalised economy, faced with which nation-states are relatively powerless. As we will see, this sows the seed for what has been called a representation or political legitimacy crisis.

In short, there is still the transformation of time. In societies that are becoming modern, the future acquires more importance than the past. Societies that are becoming modern, observes Peter Sloterdijk, become kinetic and movement in them seems to regulate everything, since they are societies locked up in a future time whose factions are unknown (Sloterdijk, 2020). Time therefore becomes performative and is experienced through movement and change. As we will see with Chilean society, the self-understanding of more traditional societies that was anchored in the past has today been weakened and chains of a short-term nature have been broken (Giddens, 1990).

These factors seem to be present in every society that has become modern from the seventeenth century to the present day. Are they present in Chile? We can speculate that yes, they are. The protests in Chile were not simply a radical or class-based riot encouraged by the regulatory intentions of justice. They also have traits that indicate that a cultural and long-term discontent was behind them.

Of course, it is not sufficient to just identify these factors to explain discontent such as that in contemporary Chile. As we saw at the beginning, a social system is the result of a group of universal factors (which I have already examined) and a unique situation that is specific to its society. We can now then ask about the factors that explain the features and emergence of discontent in Chile.

The uniqueness of discontent in Chile

As we saw at the beginning, what is occurring in Chile cannot be explained without talking about what is perhaps the most relevant phenomenon of the last fifty years: the change in the material conditions of existence of the Chilean population.[1]

Chilean society has experienced improvements in its material opportunities that would have been unimaginable for the previous generation. The memories of millions of Chileans involve a working-class past compared to a present with relative access to consumer goods. Chileans today live better and are more equal among themselves than ever before, especially according to the usual indicators (access to consumer goods, better wages, the expansion of education, etc.). However, qualitative studies and experience have gradually come to show that, on an everyday basis, people's lives hide growing symptoms of discontent (UNDP, 2017).

What is the reason behind this discontent that so stubbornly and angrily seems to accompany material improvement? According to the debate in the days after October 2019, the root of this phenomenon was mainly inequality. As scholars, public figures and television programmes have insisted with glee, Chilean society was like a balloon inflated with the air of inequality that soon burst. Other explanations have reconstructed discontent in a strictly normative way as a demand for constitutional change. There are those who have highlighted a certain illegitimacy of the elite and institutions. Other studies, however, pay attention to the fact that modernisation – understood as the commercial streamlining of life – has not managed to permeate the subjectivity of people who have not been able to recognise themselves in it.

All these explanations – or the majority of them – highlight a certain failure of the process of modernisation that took place over the last three decades, that for polemic purposes has been presented as synonymous of the neoliberal model. However, as I will suggest, there are reasons to think that the discontent in Chilean society is also the product of modernisation and the result of the processes that material modernisation itself inevitably triggers. Of course, these processes may be the subject of moral and political evaluation, as has frequently occurred in Chile, or can be reconstructed in hindsight as normative or political rejections. However, they can also be the subject of a purely descriptive literature-based social analysis, which is what I will do now.

The paradox of wellbeing and the greatest life lesson of inequality

In his study *The Old Regime and the French Revolution* (2008), Alexis de Tocqueville, one of the shrewdest observers of modern society, noted that the revolution happened suddenly because for the French, 'yoke became most unbearable where it was in fact least burdensome' (Tocqueville, 2008: 36). This can be called Tocqueville's paradox: when material wellbeing increases, expectations change and what seemed reasonable yesterday becomes insufferable today. Indeed, when wellbeing improves, expectations change and what has been as easy as breathing before becomes unbearable. This paradox has several versions, something Dr. Samuel Johnson, James Boswell testifies, noticed very early on. Boswell confirms that Dr. Johnson used to say that 'life is a progress from want to want, not from enjoyment to enjoyment' (Boswell, 2009: 607). What Johnson was trying to say is that when human life evolves and grows, its hunger – or, in more sociological terms, its expectations – change. Marx would have agreed with Dr. Johnson: when the material conditions of existence change, there is also a huge change in the culture. As he used to like saying, man only takes on problems he knows how to solve. In his manifesto – after praising the transformative power of capitalist modernisation – Marx indicates that, once this occurs, man is forced to consider his conditions of existence and his reciprocal relationships with disillusionment.

This phenomenon – which could be called the Dr. Johnson syndrome – consists of material modernisation changing people's expectations, to the extent that today our situation is the complete opposite to what was diagnosed in the 1970s by the Chilean economist Aníbal Pinto. In a famous article, Pinto indicated that Chile's problem was that it had a political system that heightened expectations but an economic system that was incapable of satisfying them (Pinto, 1970). It can therefore be said that, in 2019, before the pandemic threw everything into confusion, Chile was experiencing a similar kind of weakness but in reverse, with an economic system that encouraged consumerism and helped erase the external signs of status, but with institutions and rules that did not coincide with the assumptions underlying this very same economic system.

To describe it in Hegelian terms, Chilean society does not live up to its reality. Hegel thought there was a normative pattern behind modern society, its contradictions and the equality between these that struggled to get out. Something similar seems to be happening in Chile: capitalist modernisation has generalised the normative patterns used to judge its institutions and people therefore want Chilean society to live up to reality. In simpler terms, as a result of capitalist modernisation, there is a culture inspired by the meritocratic fantasy, according to which the fairest society is the one whose distribution is in proportion to personal effort but which, in many aspects, resists doing so. Is this not perhaps the reason for the complaints about the educational system: that it is more sensitive to people's birthplace than their actual efforts? Is this not the same underlying reason for the complaints against a credit system that cheats people, not making their effort worthwhile?

In the twentieth century, the paradox that has just been referred to was explained in terms that were a little more technical, although the underlying idea is exactly the same. One of those explanations belongs to Fred Hirsch and emerges from the concept of positional goods. These kinds of goods – for example educational certificates – have a useful function that is not related to the number of them a person has. A university degree is one of those goods and the wellbeing it provides is greater the fewer the number of people who have them. This explains why the widespread increase in goods and consumerism specific to modern societies – from statutory goods such as cars to other more symbolic ones like university degrees – only brings frustration instead of satisfaction (Hirsch, 2005). Pierre Bourdieu detected this in the phenomenon he called the 'hysteresis effect' (a word that comes from the Greek, meaning to arrive late). He explained that what occurs is that the historically excluded masses hope to find an aura of prestige and the high wages they admire from a distance in goods such as education. When they had them though, they discovered that this aura that had turned them into actual substitutes for noble titles had disappeared and vanished as a result of widespread access (Bourdieu, 2000: 140). Therefore, although something is easier to access, it brings with it a great sense of frustration.

Psychoanalysis also provides some explanations. Capitalism – and what Chile has lived through is a capitalist modernisation – connects pleasure and enjoyment to consumerism and merchandise. The *object to* (as psychoanalysts call the object that acts as a catalyst for desire) is like what is inside the 'Kinder Surprise' chocolate eggs – a small toy, a message, a small plastic object in a vacuum. The desire around which social life is centred is a permanently deferred promise and the bad news is that this is specific to any kind of social education (Žižek, 2003: 145ff). The ongoing expansion of consumerism (and the chance to buy more Kinder Surprises in the hope that the next one will have the toy you want) is a way of staunching inequality, as is the promise the meritocratic educational system offers of mobility. However, if consumerism stops spreading or the education system does not provide a structure that makes merit reputable, the wound of inequality begins to bleed. Something similar to this is what has started to happen in Chile.

Related to the paradox of wellbeing is what is the greatest show of inequality. Among the different factors that explain the phenomenon of an increase in experiencing inequality (despite its relative decrease) is what Amartya Sen has identified as positional objectivity. What is interesting about this concept is the fact that it helps us understand the paradox of wellbeing that Tocqueville highlighted very early on in the middle of the nineteenth century (around the same time as Marx coined his theory about 'objective illusion').

We usually think that objectivity is a quality of the opinions whose validity or worth does not depend on the position and characteristics of the person who emits them. However, it seems obvious that, in order to form beliefs and justify actions, objectivity is positionally dependent (Sen, 2009: 157). A group of people can share a handful of beliefs as a result of their positions, even though a thorough trans-positional assessment shows that they are wrong (Sen, 1993: 130). Sen has suggested, therefore, that positional objectivity is equivalent to what Marx called 'objective illusion'.

The way of legitimising inequality

Another factor that has undoubtedly contributed to the phenomenon of growing discontent is the relative failure of how inequality is legitimised. As Max Weber highlights, happy human beings believe they have the right to happiness and unhappy people deserve to be in the situation they are in (Weber, 2002: 393). This is where the legitimisation of inequality comes in as one of the key aspects of social life.

All societies have an unequal distribution of prestige, power and wealth, which is why the issue of stratification is one of sociology's favourite topics. The question that is worth formulating is not so much about whether this is unequal or not or to what extent (this is an important question but of a moral nature), but rather how and through which mechanisms or by generalising which fantasies inequality can be legitimised.

It is well known that the social sciences have long used the concept of ideology to allude to the phantom cover we use to represent reality to ourselves. From the cosmic vision used to represent the system of castes in India to the meritocratic idea Michael Young caricatured (Young, 1958), all societies have a story to explain their differences. Although Marxism believed it saw in these structures a false consciousness that we could sometimes get rid of, it is most likely that this forms a part of culture and of the multiple ways human beings make themselves comfortable in the midst of reality. Quoting T.S. Elliot, we could say that societies have ideologies because 'no one can bear so much reality'. Social reality comes to us surrounded by certain phantom covers that legitimise it and allow us to accept it. Therefore, capitalist modernisation – or capitalism in general – is legitimised by the promise of consumerism's permanent spread and by the idea that resources are distributed in proportion to the effort made to obtain them and the talent shown. In the case of Chile, both legitimising mechanisms have faced serious setbacks. The educational reform, which is one of the most effective ways T.H. Marshall suggests of legitimising inequality

(Marshall, 1965: 76ff), never managed to shape a meritocratic system or one that was plausibly meritocratic. Consumerism, for its part, ended up breaking one of the promises made by the right-wing government that had come to power less than two years before the riots. In other words, the main validating aspect of modernisation – the fantasy that envelopes it – was ripped open and, when looking through the gap that was left, only simple contingency could be seen, encouraging the increase in voluntarism seen since October 2019.

Anomie and the generational issue

In general terms, the word 'anomie' describes a kind of lapsus in the normative regulation of behaviour. In the work of Durkheim, who came up with the concept, this phenomenon describes both individual and social disorders (Lockwood, 2000: 69). Referring to this phenomenon's social dimension, this author uses the expression 'disqualification'. He suggests that every society classifies social positions and tasks, giving them a certain amount of resources to which they can legitimately aspire (Durkheim, 2005: 210). However, when transformations occur that are 'too sudden (whether due to painful crises or happy changes)', disqualification and a time of inevitable disorganisation suddenly occurs.

> Time is required for the public conscience to reclassify men and things. So long as the social forces thus freed have not regained equilibrium, their respective values are unknown and so all regulation is lacking for a time. The limits are unknown between the possible and the impossible, what is just and what is unjust, legitimate claims and hopes and those which are immoderate. Consequently, there is no restraint upon aspirations.
>
> (Durkheim, 2005: 213)

In the rapid modernisation Chile experienced, it is not difficult to see examples of the disillusionment that Durkheim describes. However, as we have just been reminded, anomie does not only have a social dimension (which, as we have seen, Durkheim describes as 'disillusionment'). It also has a dimension at the level of how people behave, which translates into a lack of normative orientation.

Modernisation usually weakens the most immediate branches of socialisation, such as the family, church or neighbourhood. When this occurs – and this has undoubtedly happened in Chile to an extent – the normative orientation of action declines and individuals are left alone with their subjectivity. This phenomenon was described by Arnold Gehlen regarding the place of institutions in the human condition. It is worth remembering this author's main idea for understanding what sociology describes as anomie. He suggests that the human animal is characterised by what he called 'pulsional excess'. When they do not have a biologically established behaviour, the man or woman needs to get rid of that pulsional excess, repress their subjectivity, save effort by establishing a routine for their behaviour and, in this way, stabilise their interaction. This set of functions is carried out by institutions (Gehlen, 1988: 56). Understood like this, institutions do not have the function of *externally* regulating behaviour but rather, where they exist and function, behaviour is configured *from inside*. Institutions also model ways of experiencing the world, the values pursued, emotions and voluntary actions. Surprising as it sounds, human beings trade, work, give orders or obey, pray and establish emotional bonds within an institution, whether the market, family, political system or church. Without institutions, they live in a permanent state of change, with no chance to brood (Ortega and Gasset, 2006: 527).

Therefore, when institutions are weakened and when society, in Durkheim's words, is disillusioned – what happened in Chile as a result of rapid modernisation – what can be described as a motivational outbreak occurs, a term literature has used for a long time when referring to riots and large-scale phenomena. As we immediately see though, the way to describe this kind of process is not as anomie. From the 1980s onwards, a lot of literature has questioned the factors that, in contemporary societies, lead to protests and give them their distinctive appearance. Almost all of this describes what can be called a kind of cultural contradiction, with the diverse traits of the protests a sample of this.

The protest's cultural dimension

It is sufficient to take a look at the streets of Santiago – or even to have witnessed the protests from a distance – to notice two things that, to the unprepared observer, jump right out: there was nothing organic behind them, nor an ideological programme guiding them. Instead, a wide range of demands that was more than radical – and more than indicating something about what has been relinquished – seemed to show that there was a widespread desire to change the world. The huge march that brought together more than a million people in Santiago immediately after the events of October showed how diverse the protest's origins were. At times, it seemed more like a crowd of individuals and groups than a mass. From the midst of it emerged intangible demands, a longing for recognition, the politics of identity and the desire to reshape the sense of their own lives socially. To what then did this movement owe its strong desire to shape culture? Literature gives us a clue. From the 1980s onwards, it is remarkable to see that social movements in capitalist societies started to acquire a cultural aspect that distanced them from the issue of class as classic Marxism prescribed, or from merely laying claim to interests that group action tried to explain. Jürgen Habermas, for example, observed that these kinds of conflict do not emerge in the area of material reproduction, nor are they channelled in the party system or restrained by the specific compensation offered by the system. They do, however, emerge in the areas of cultural reproduction or social integration. This problem is relative to the 'grammar of life forms' and appears in the seams joining the highly abstract social system with the sphere of meaning of the life world. It is worth quoting what he observed:

> Alternative praxis is opposed to the profit-oriented instrumentalization of professional labour, the market-dependent mobilisation of labour, the extension of competitiveness and performance pressure into elementary school. It is also directed against the process whereby services, relations and time become monetary values, against the consumerist redefinition of private life spheres and personal life styles. . . . The partial dissolution of the social roles of employees and consumers, of clients and citizens, should, according to the programmatic conceptions of some theoreticians, clear the path for counter-institutions developed from within the life-world in order to limit the particular dynamic of the economic and political-administrative system of action.
>
> (Habermas, 1981: 36–37)

This struggle for the 'grammar of forms of life' – as this author called it – helps us understand the emotional component of new social movements. Exaggerated versions of the protests and performances that turn citizens into the audience – phenomena that were seen in Santiago – not only are strategic resources but also reflect the values and non-discursive elements that underlie emerging cultures (Flam and King, 2005).

The availability of resources in societies going through modernisation invites individuals to fulfil their potential but, at the same time, involves a multitude of abstract organisations that regulate and control almost all aspects of individuals' lives. Alberto Melucci has therefore described participants in these new movements as 'nomads of the present', since their ways of organising themselves and their practices are not only a means but also an end in themselves. Melucci's observation is particularly significant when it comes to the fact that many of these movements – with the exception of the use of a certain imagery that Marx noticed in his Eighteenth Brumaire – are obviously disconnected from the past, breaking the transient nature of the chain (Melucci, 1980, 1989). Other authors like Alain Touraine

(1985, 1994) and Daniel Bell (1996) have pointed out the same phenomenon. There is a rift or cultural contradiction in modern capitalism, stimulating the spontaneity of the 'I' and the self-editing of one's own life but, at the same time, demanding technical logic to make wellbeing possible. In all of this, Touraine detected an awareness of historicity that modern capitalism cannot satisfy through its own structure. This revealed itself in modernism as an aesthetic movement very early on. There is the suspicion that, underneath the rationalised and technical world, beats a contradictory reality that is struggling to come out.

In his studies on contemporary culture, Frederic Jameson suggests that this contradictory reality produced a 'breakdown of the signifying chain', following a Jacques Lacan's idea. It is well known that, for Sassure (who Lacan follows), meaning does not come from the relationship between the signifier and the reality it signifies, but rather is derived from the relationship of one signifier with others. When this chain is broken, sense disappears. Therefore, young people appear to experience a 'breakdown of the signifying chain' and do not today manage to unify the present, the past and the future in the same experience. Breaking with this transient nature frees the present from all the meanings it is a carrier of and, after it has been freed, it becomes intense, with 'a mysterious charge of affect, here described in the negative terms of anxiety and loss of reality, but which one could just as well imagine in the positive terms of euphoria, a high, an intoxicatory or hallucinogenic intensity' (Jameson, 1991: 27–28).

Similar assessments can be found in Chilean literature. Araujo and Martuccelli (2012) have suggested in their research that modernisation and the appearance of abstract systems are experienced as distant impositions that do not make sense:

> Whatever the strengths of neoliberalism – insofar as the ideology of the main political players (and the ruling elite) – this ideology is far from defines the effective content of the majority of Chileans' political and historical conscience.
> Araujo and Martuccelli, 2012: I, 71)

Martuccelli and Araujo's research closely follows a hypothesis formulated at the turn of the century by Manuel Antonio Garretón, who said that a process exists that is, to a certain extent, contradictory. In this, rationalised and capitalist modernisation based on the model of the nation-state's industrial society intertwines with the emergence of local and community belongings that tend to exacerbate emotions' subjectivity. The setting-up of the subject, which is the key issue of modernity, occurs amid the contradiction between expression and rationalisation. Faced with a type of society that is completely 'modern', Garretón observes that even ascriptive, traditional or religious elements tend to lose their natural, atavistic and meta-social dimensions and become historical subjects (Garretón, 2000: 44).

In the light of this rapid literature review, it is easy to conclude that Chilean society's discontent has a meaning that goes beyond the explicit normative significance some give to it, when it is asserted that this discontent is caused by demands for constitutional change and for greater equality. It is likely that this normative meaning is the ex post rationalisation of a discontent whose causes that can be better described as imbalances between subjectivity and structure. This, of course, does not invalidate the normative demands, but it does not help to have too much confidence in the therapeutic results some people during the debate have usually assigned to it. As we have seen, discontent in modernising societies seems to have causes that go further than – or, depending on how you look at it, are closer to – the normative demands political players assign them. In modernising societies, there is apparently an underlying discontent – the old *malaise* – which is expressed over and over again through the intervals uncovered by the rationalisation of life, regulated in different ways by the rationalisation the elite are capable of imprinting on the compass of political opportunity (Yack, 1986). This *malaise* does not, of course, have specific normative content but rather sources that keep feeding it and promising to cure it: subjectivity and memory.

Changes in the political cleavage

One of the mysteries that have accompanied discontent in Chile is that it manifested itself widely and violently barely eighteen months after the right won the presidential elections. This was extremely surprising because something like this had only happened once before (under Jorge Alessandri in 1958) during the whole of the twentieth century; now, in the twenty-first century, it had already happened twice (with the figure of Piñera in 2010 and 2018). It is true that electoral participation had been low, but this is normal in comparative systems. The fact is that the right won an unprecedented victory among active citizens (the same who, up to then, had preferred the centre-left and who would rebel in October soon afterwards).

What explains such a brusque change in the active electorate? One explanation could be the change in the political cleavage. Political scientists call cleavage those divisions around which political preferences are articulated. Early on in the work of Marx and Weber, a connection was made between social divides (of class or status) and political divides. In other words, people align themselves politically depending on their real or imagined social situation.

Later on, influential political scientists (for instance, Lipset and Rokkan, 1967) identified class conflicts as key to political divides. In modern democracies, they said, the conflict between different groups is expressed through political parties that basically represent the democratic translation of the class struggle. Subsequent academic contributions have identified several other divides that the political struggle depends on, such as religious, ethnic or regional divides.

What has happened in Chile regarding cleavage? During the nineteenth century, religious divides shaped the party system, particularly the Catholic Church's opposing opinion to society on matters such as education or culture. During the twentieth century, this cleavage came to look similar to what Lipset and Rokkan described, with class structure guiding the political divide. This was the so-called 'state of compromise' (1932–1970), where the middle class and the political centre were at the middle of the balance, which sometimes governed with the right and sometimes with the left. It was at the end of the Pinochet regime in the late 1980s when the cleavage started to change radically. The class divide was replaced by the divide between authoritarianism and democracy and this guided Chilean politics until well into the twenty-first century.

Taken advantage of heavily by the centre-left, it is possible that this divide has changed as a result of modernisation itself and the material conditions of existence. The spread of consumerism and changes in life trajectories over more than two decades may have led to a change in preferences, together with a disengagement from politics. Therefore, the right's electoral victory was not ideological but rather just one more expression of how lightweight political preferences had become in a society in which, as a result of the material spread of consumerism, people journey towards a status that distances them from their class position. The right, however, had misunderstood their electoral victory, believing it to be ideological. They did not realise that it involved a fluid and circumstantial adaptation, the result of a swift divide that was closely connected to what was on offer in the elections.

The legitimacy of institutions

The Chilean state has always gained legitimacy retrospectively (using images built up by historiography), turning to the idea of the nation. During the twentieth century, it did so by adopting the form of the 'state of compromise', an arrangement based on the middle class that tended to resolve the social issue of the twentieth century: incorporating the urban proletariat.

What is happening to the state today? What seems to be occurring is that it has entered into a crisis as far as these two dimensions are concerned. To put it another way, Chilean society's self-understanding is changing. When Chile's situation is examined in a broader Latin American context, what usually stands out is that Chile was the first country in the region that managed to consolidate its state, thanks to the army's early modernisation and the successful wars conducted against its neighbours, among other factors. Due to a deliberate process of sustained acculturation, it was also the first state in Latin America to be able to spread a shared awareness of its own origins successfully. This acculturation led to a powerful national consciousness that, for its part, created a population that was loyal to the state, consolidating by this its legitimacy. Nowadays, Chilean society's self-understanding is in crisis or in the process of changing, revealing its contingencies. The idea of nation as an immemorial community of blood and soil, constructed by the state during the nineteenth century and a good part of the twentieth century, is being substituted by the rebirth of a local sense of belonging and cultures, drowned out by the hegemony of the nation-state.

Political modernity, above all, has emerged in close connection with the idea of a nation as a community whose roots are submerged in the past and whose members recognise a shared origin. In the case of Chile, this idea was the result of a long process of deliberate acculturation carried out by the state, the school system, the Catholic Church, universities, imagery and republican rites. It achieved a very polished narrative in the self-understanding that historiography spread in the twenty-first century. The Chilean nation is therefore the result of the cultural homogenisation carried out by the state in order to create citizens loyal to its institutions.

According to some studies (cf. CIIR, 2020), these images already lack symbolic effectiveness among the Chilean population. The overwhelming majority conceive Chilean society as a multicultural or multi-nation entity. Around 90 per cent of this study's sample supports constitutional recognition for the indigenous people and a large majority define Chilean society as multicultural. To put it another way, Chile is moving from the *ethnos* to the *demos*. This move from a timeless community (*ethnos*) to a purely political one (*demos*) poses special challenges. Of course, the main one is how to thoughtfully shape a social connection or link between groups and people who do not recognise that they have a common past. This deteriorates state legitimacy. Without an imagined community to sustain it, the state loses the abstract link that allows it to generate trust and demand obedience.

The legitimacy of the state and its institutions arises from two sources: goods and services benefits on one hand and citizen preferences on the other. Nowadays, it is very difficult to satisfy both sources of legitimacy (cf. Rosanvallon, 2011). As seen by events in October 2019, citizen demands are extremely heterogeneous and diverse and many of them have a definite generational and cultural aspect that the state is not able to satisfy. The idea that social demands are simply vindictive or class related is wrong. This makes it very hard for the state to act as a provider of goods and services. On the other hand, as we have already seen, representing the majority is also very difficult in a political culture whose cleavage has broken away from the social structure and seems to be closer to individuation and the perception of status.

The result of all this is that institutional legitimacy is visibly deteriorated, therefore creating an environment of opportunities for the buried discontent specific to modern societies to manifest in the form of an increasing number of protests and calls to break with the establishment.

The changes in political culture: final remarks

One of the truths that have been firmly established in the social sciences since Marx formulated it in his 1859 'Preface to A Critique of Political Economy' is that changes to the material conditions of existence modify culture sooner or later.

> The mode of production of material life conditions the social, political, and intellectual life process in general. It is not the consciousness of men that determines their being, but, on the contrary, their social being that determines their consciousness.
>
> (Marx, 2000: 424–425)

What changes can be seen in the culture of a society like Chile's, which has experienced the process of material change with both the advantages and disadvantages I have just examined?

As already seen, Chilean society's ability of self-understanding that guided it during the twentieth century has been seriously deteriorated. The imagined community, amid which the idea of nation unfolded, has been significantly weakened. In its place, a variety of different ways of life are flourishing, one of which involves the politics of identity, something that is gaining ground in the public space. In addition, elective autonomy and identities have expanded, as well as a weakening of social connections that is felt as a loss of cohesion. We can therefore speculate that Chilean society is in the middle of a challenge to rework its understanding of itself, which itself is the basis for social ties.

Organised modernity (Wagner, 1994) based on the nation-state, the class structure and culture has given way to a growing awareness of how conventional or contingent social life is. This phenomenon can be seen in Chile. All of a sudden, the possibility of a social life has been laid bare and will demand a place in shaping lives. It can be speculated that this phenomenon has led to two processes: a change in the normative guidelines that are used to judge distribution in social life, and a drive to rework social connections reflexively.

The change in normative guidelines

The political culture of contemporary societies is characterised by stripping away any claims to natural and social inheritance when distributing resources and opportunities. This trait of political culture is the exact opposite to the individual autonomy that underpins the institutions of modern societies, democracy and human rights. Individual autonomy rests on the idea that each man or woman is the agent of their own trajectory and, for that same reason, has certain responsibilities. In other words, this ideal fuels the demand for justice faced with any kind of privilege that depends on where you were born or the distribution of purely natural talent (which is obviously considered undeserved). The natural distribution of gifts such as intelligence or physical capabilities or the inheritance that each person receives from birth as a portion of social or cultural capital is not deemed sufficient to justify said distribution. This is what is specific to the political culture of contemporary societies: taking away all authority from nature and history and instead transferring it to will (Peña, 2020c).

This explains why, when classic authors characterise the transition towards a modern society, they describe this as a step *from status to contract*. However, contemporary societies – and this phenomenon is seen to a great extent in contemporary Chile – do not take long to point out that choice has shaped itself both culturally and historically. These societies also realise that the diverse processes of subjectivation – that depend on gender, ethnicity or sexual orientation – have established important differences between individuals. Abstract citizenship and the demands for justice that reject any ascriptive trait are therefore substituted by an awareness of factors that establish undeserved disadvantages and that need to be corrected. This phenomenon gives way to what has been called identity politics. The individual therefore begins to argue that belonging to a group is the reason for their demands or for their political position.

In other words, if the transition towards modern society is characterised as a journey from status to contract, there is in the public sphere nowadays a *return to status* in the form of an identity politics. Seeds of this phenomenon have already begun to be sown in present-day Chile, particularly in the recently formed Constitutional Convention. On the one hand, modern society demands for individuality which is at the basis of some of its institutions, such as the market. On the other hand, however, modern society also experiences how the awareness of a collective identity is shaking up memory, changing the nation's self-understanding and playing down individual autonomy. Chilean society today is in the middle of this dilemma.

The thoughtful reworking of social connections

The crisis that I have examined in this chapter can be described as a fissure between people's expectations and the experience they have access to through the institutions that regulate social life. This gap between expectations and experience can only be resolved by readjusting the latter, changing institutions and the rules on how they model the distribution of opportunities and resources. The path the modern political order knows to do this is constitutional change. Chile is at the beginning of a constitutional change that aims to make institutions live up to the regulatory direction and demands of Chilean society today. The first weeks of this experience have revealed the main challenges that need to be faced. It is worth briefly mentioning three of these. One is how identity politics will be approached, not to be confused with the demand for recognition for native people. Another is how certain essential basic goods will be distributed to ensure an equal distribution of the agency capabilities of the individuals, formulated as the demand for social rights. The third involves distributing the risk of illness and old age in a way that does not depend on performance or prior contributions.

The convention's first debates have already revealed that the old idea of nation forged under the auspices of nineteenth-century historiography has made way for a multicultural nation whose main challenge is subsequently to elaborate its own memory in a way that makes sense to contemporary audiences. The distribution of basic goods, for example, needs to be compatible with constitutional rules on this matter, opening up an opportunity for a democratic policy that, according to the rules, agrees on the most efficient way of satisfying this. On the other hand, distributing the cost of illness and old age will involve balancing universalist policies with contributory ones.

Resolving these three basic problems, though, will not ensure that discontent fades away. As we have seen, discontent has deeper roots than normative or legal demands. As Raymond Aron once shrewdly observed, societies that modernise – that have to coordinate autonomy and authority, rationalisation and spontaneity, equality and differences and identity and performance – seem condemned to live in an inevitable struggle between progress and disillusionment (Aron, 1968, 1989).

Note

1 Here I refer to what I have analysed in greater detail in the book *Pensar el malestar* (Santiago, Taurus, 2020a) and in the article 'La revolución inhallable', *Estudios Públicos* 158: 7–29 (2020b).

References

Araujo, K. and D. Martuccelli (2012) *Desafíos comunes: Retrato de la sociedad chilena y sus individuos (volume 1)*. Santiago: LOM.
Aron, R. (1968) *Progress and Disillusion: The Dialectics of Modern Society*. London: Pall Mall.
Aron, R. (1989) 'Relato, análisis, interpretación, explicación: Crítica de algunos problemas del conocimiento histórico', in R. Aron (ed.) *Estudios sociológicos*, pp. 87–141. Madrid: Espasa-Calpe.
Bell, D. (1996) *The Cultural Contradictions of Capitalism*. New York: Basic Books.
Boswell, J. (2009) *The Life of Samuel Johnson*. London: Penguin Classics.
Bourdieu, P. (2000) *La distinción: Criterio y bases sociales del gusto*. Madrid: Taurus.
CIIR (2020) *Estudios de opinión pública. Segunda medición: Pueblos originarios y nueva constitución*. Santiago: Centro de Estudios Interculturales e Indígenas.
Dancy, J. (2000) *Practical Reality*. Oxford: Clarendon Press.
Durkheim, E. (2005) *Suicide*. London: Routledge.
Flam, H. and D. King (eds.) (2005) *Emotions and Social Movements*. London: Routledge.
Garretón, M.A. (2000) *La sociedad en que vivi(re)mos: Introducción sociológica al cambio de siglo*. Santiago: LOM.
Gehlen, A. (1988) *The Man: His Nature and Place in the World*. New York: Columbia University Press.
Giddens, A. (1990) *The Consequences of Modernity*. Cambridge: Polity Press.
Habermas, J. (1981) 'New Social Movements', *Telos* 49: 33–37.
Hirsch, F. (2005) *Social Limits to Growth*. London: Routledge.
Jameson, F. (1991) *Postmodernism or, the Cultural Logic of Late Capitalism*. Durham: Duke University Press.
Lipset, S.M. and S. Rokkan (eds.) (1967) *Party Systems and Voter Alignments*. New York: Free Press.
Lockwood, D. (2000) *Solidarity and Schism*. Oxford: Clarendon Press.
Luhmann, N. (1990) *Political Theory in the Welfare State*. Berlin and New York: Walter de Gruyter.
Luhmann, N. (2007) *La Sociedad de la sociedad*. Mexico City: Herder.
Marshall, T.H. (1965) *Class, Citizenship, and Social Development*. New York: Anchor Books.
Marx, K. (2000) 'Preface to a Critique of Political Economy', in D. McLellan (ed.) *Karl Marx Selected Writings*, pp. 424–428. Oxford: Oxford University Press.
MDSF (2019) *Desarrollo Social 2019*. Santiago: Ministerio de desarrollo social y familia.
Melucci, A. (1980) 'The New Social Movements: A Theoretical Approach', *Theory and Methods/ Théorie and Méthodes* 19(2): 199–226.
Melucci, A. (1989) *Nomads of the Present: Social Movements and Individual Needs in Contemporary Society*. Philadelphia: Temple University Press.
Ortega y Gasset, J. (2006) 'Ensimismamiento y alteración', in J. Ortega y Gasset (ed.) *Obras Completas*, vol. 5, pp. 529–550. Madrid: Taurus.

Parsons, T. (2021) *The Social Systems*. New Orleans: Quid Pro Books.
Peña, C. (2020a) *Pensar el malestar: Sobre la crisis de octubre y la cuestión constitucional*. Santiago: Taurus.
Peña, C. (2020b) 'La revolución inhallable', *Estudios Públicos* 158: 7–29.
Peña, C. (2020c) *La mentira noble: Sobre el lugar del mérito en la vida humana*. Santiago: Taurus.
Pinto, A. (1970) 'Desarrollo económico y relaciones sociales', in A. Pinto *et al.* (eds.) *Chile Hoy*, pp. 5–52. Mexico City: Siglo XXI.
Rosanvallon, P. (2011) *La legitimidad democrática: Imparcialidad, reflexividad y proximidad*. Buenos Aires: Paidós.
Sapelli, C. (2016) *Chile: ¿Más equitativo? Una mirada a la dinámica social del Chile de ayer, hoy y mañana*. Santiago: Ediciones UC.
Sen, A. (1993) 'Positional Objectivity', *Philosophy and Public Affairs* 22(2): 126–145.
Sen, A. (2009) *Idea of Justice*. Cambridge, MA: Harvard University Press.
Simmel, G. (1991) 'Money in Modern Culture', *Theory, Culture and Society* 8: 17–31.
Simmel, G. (2000) 'The Concept and Tragedy of Culture', in D. Frisby and M. Featherstone (eds.) *Simmel on Culture*, pp. 55–75. London: Sage.
Sloterdijk, P. (2020) *Infinite Mobilization*. Cambridge: Polity Press.
Starobinski, J. (1971) *Jean Jacques Rousseau: La transparence et l'obstacle*. Paris: Gallimard.
Tocqueville, A. de (2008) *The Ancient Regimen and the Revolution*. London: Penguin Classics.
Touraine, A. (1985) 'An Introduction to the Study of Social Movements', *Social Research* 52(4): 749–787.
Touraine, A. (1994) *Crítica de la modernidad*. Buenos Aires: Fondo de Cultura Económica.
UNDP (2017) *Desiguales. Orígenes, cambios y desafíos de la brecha social en Chile*. Santiago: Uqbar.
UNDP (2019) *Informe sobre Desarrollo Humano 2019. Más allá del ingreso, más allá de los promedios, más allá del presente: Desigualdades del desarrollo humano en el siglo XXI*. Santiago: United Nations Development Programme.
Wagner, P. (1994) *Sociology of Modernity: Liberty and Discipline*. London: Routledge.
Weber, M. (2002) *Economía y Sociedad: Esbozo de sociología comprensiva*. Mexico City: Fondo de Cultura Económica.
World Bank (2020) *World Development Indicators Database*. Washington: The World Bank.
Yack, B. (1986) *The Longing for Total Revolution: Philosophic Sources of Social Discontent from Rousseau to Marx and Nietzsche*. Princeton: Princeton University Press.
Young, M. (1958) *The Rise of the Meritocracy 1870–2033: An Essay on Education and Society*. London: Thames and Hudson.
Žižek, S. (2003) *The Puppet and the Dwarf: The Perverse Core of Christianity*. Boston: MIT Press.

2 The October rebellion
Exploring its historical roots

Patricio Silva

Introduction

Following the events of October 18th 2019, several political analysts have knuckled down to try and get to the bottom of the main causes of the so-called social uprising in Chile since, from that day forward, the country has been embroiled in one of the greatest political-institutional crises of its history. The October rebellion was undoubtedly the result of numerous historical, economic, political, social and cultural factors that cannot be captured easily in a single academic essay. In addition, the roots of these factors do not date back to recent times. That is why any attempt to try and explain the reasons for the October riots and the subsequent institutional crisis that occurred in the country requires a long-term historical perspective. Particular attention must be paid to the impact that the Unidad Popular government (1970–1973) and Pinochet's long dictatorship (1973–1990) still have on the current political process. This is because what happened during that turbulent period of history has conditioned the actions of the country's different political sectors up to the present today.

In this chapter, I explore the evolution of two cleavages that have had a profound effect on Chile's political evolution in the last half century. Under the Unidad Popular government and the military dictatorship, the old right-left cleavage became unusually confrontational. In addition, the dramatic end of Allende's government and Pinochet's subsequent neoliberal revolution created a deep cleavage between the radical and moderate sectors in the left itself, something that still has a major impact on the current political scenario. In my opinion, both of these political rifts have played a decisive role in the unusual radicalisation experienced by the Chilean left from 2010 onwards, eventually resulting in the October 2019 uprising. In other words, the left's intense radicalisation has, in my opinion, been key to enabling other factors to come together and produce the October 18th uprising. Both the October rebellion and the insurrectionary and rupturist scenario that

DOI: 10.4324/9781003254355-3

ensued would have been unthinkable without the extreme radicalisation that the Chilean left experienced between 2010 and 2019.

The 'mono-polarisation' of the Chilean left

Paradoxically, the notorious politicisation and radicalisation experienced from 2010 onwards by the majority of the Chilean left occurred in a society that has actually been heavily depoliticised for decades (Silva, 2004). Therefore, what has happened in Chile over the last ten years involves a previously unheard phenomenon of 'mono-polarisation'. While the left has come to adopt an ever more radical and maximalist stance, the right, on the other hand, has remained demobilised and has defended a relatively moderate one.[1]

This situation contrasts heavily with the climate of acute politicisation and radicalisation the country as a whole experienced at the beginning of the 1970s, culminating in the military coup in September 1973. During those years, the economic and social reform programmes of Allende's government created an extreme level of radicalisation and polarisation on both sides of the right-left cleavage (Valenzuela, 1978). On the one hand, the Chilean right adopted a distinctly insurrectional stance, expressed through the creation of clash groups and by initiating rebel actions that culminated in an open call to the armed forces to depose the Allende government (Pollack, 1999). A similar process occurred within the left itself, seen in the creation of combative workers' defence brigades (the so-called *cordones industriales*) and in an important radicalisation of the Unidad Popular parties' discourse and political actions. The consolidation of socialism in Chile was seen as an irreversible process that had to be defended by all possible means (Sigmund, 1977).

On the other hand, after the return to democracy in 1990, there has been a process of increasing unilateral radicalisation among the Chilean left. In my opinion, the fact that, this time, this radicalisation did not include the right is a reflection of the long and strong hegemony exerted by neoliberalism Chile since the late 1970s. The right considered itself victorious, since it managed to impose a political, economic and institutional system that seemed to have been consolidated (Vergara, 1985; Gárate, 2012). It was exactly this reality that I believe ended up exasperating broad sectors of the left. As a result of Sebastián Piñera's victory in 2010, the left began to make use of diverse political strategies, including organising violent street protests, to try and prevent by any means possible the consolidation of neoliberalism in the country.

Until 2010, the right had not needed to adopt a more defensive stance. At that time, the anti-systemic left was a minority and did not seem to have much capacity for political and social mobilisation. The right knew that both the economic system and the existing legislation were protected by the so-called 'política de acuerdos' struck by the Concertación governments. Even after the emergence of the student movement in 2011, the right continued to believe for a long time that the status quo was not in danger. They based this on the fact that the well-functioning economy and the country's strong political institutions would continue to protect the political-institutional apparatus on which the free market system was based.

During the Concertación governments, however, a feeling of discontent among the moderate left that was part of this coalition became more and more evident. This sector eventually internalised and accepted the ongoing criticism they received from the Communist Party, the Revolutionary Left Movement (MIR) and other extreme left groups. The radical left criticised the social-democratic left for apparently having become a mere administrator of the neoliberal model inherited from the military regime. In reality, however, the Concertación governments introduced profound reforms to the neoliberal system, as seen in an important expansion of state presence and a broad set of robust social policies.

Sebastián Piñera's right-wing government, which came to power in 2010, put an end to the long twenty-year cycle of Concertación governments. This was a dramatic turning point as far as the left's position on the economic model and institutional apparatus inherited from the 1980 Constitution was concerned. From this moment onwards, the memory of the fall of Allende's government and the seventeen years of military dictatorship started to fuel the Chilean left's political discourse and emotions. For many of its members, it was unacceptable that the right, which had helped defeat the Unidad Popular government and given its complete support to Pinochet's dictatorship, was once again in power. As a result, old methods of protest and slogans that had been used in the past to fight against the military dictatorship emerged from the heart of the left. This time though, the left conducted an unyielding opposition to a government that had been legitimately elected by democratic means.

After the student protests in 2011, the Chilean left entered a new phase of accelerated radicalisation, which would cumulate years later in the October 2019 riots. The fact that the heart of the left was becoming more and more radical was clearly seen when the Nueva Mayoría coalition was created and then when it came to power in 2014. From the very beginning, Bachelet's second government promoted a notably anti-neoliberal and maximalist discourse, in which it suggested changing the very foundations of both the economic system and the constitutional architecture. The aim of wanting to put an end to the neoliberal model was graphically reflected in the controversial words of Nueva Mayoría spokesperson, Senator Jaime Quintana, when he said, 'We aren't going to steamroll over everything, we're going to use a bulldozer, because we have to destroy the obsolete foundations of the dictatorship's neoliberal model' (*El Mercurio*, 25 March 2014). In addition, the Nueva Mayoría government openly distanced itself from its own past by harshly criticising both the Concertación governments of which it had formed a part and the 'política de acuerdos' established with the right between 1990 and 2010. Quintana's declarations struck deep into the heart of the right, which saw in his declaration the true aims of the package of reforms announced by Bachelet. From then onwards, the right began to regard the Nueva Mayoría government as an attempt to revive Salvador Allende's Unidad Popular.[2]

The Nueva Mayoría coalition had the intellectual support of several left-wing scholars who, in different books and articles, began to foresee the 'imminent' end of neoliberalism in Chile. In addition, they predicted that it would inevitably be replaced by a new system based on universal social rights and new forms of citizen participation. This was the case in *El otro modelo*, written by a group of well-known scholars and intellectuals (Atría et al., 2013). This book actually offered a plan of action to carry out profound transformations in the legal-institutional area, in administering public services, in education and in other public policy areas, with the aim of putting an end to the neoliberal regime. That same year, the book *El derrumbe del modelo* by sociologist Alberto Mayol was published, presenting an almost apocalyptic image of Chilean neoliberalism which, in the author's opinion, was in its last days (Mayol, 2013).

Bachelet's second government would end up being a meagre political and economic administration, incapable of constructing a viable alternative to the neoliberalism that was dominant. This meant that most Chileans eventually rejected the eclectic and improvised reforms proposed by the Nueva Mayoría. This became obvious in the December 2017 presidential elections, when Sebastián Piñera was re-elected and the neoliberal agenda once again established in the country (Brunner, 2016; Ampuero et al., 2017; Walker, 2018).

The Nueva Mayoría government's inability to inflict a lethal blow on the neoliberal system meant that the student movement and left-wing young people in general began to adopt a stance that was more and more extreme and rupturist. Several of the leaders of the 2011 student movement threw themselves into founding new political organisations. This marked the beginning of the Frente Amplio, bringing together a group of small parties and movements that supported the use of extremely confrontational and rupturist actions against the centre-left, the right and the capitalist regime in general (Mayol and Cabrera, 2018).

In my opinion, the right's return to power in March 2018 ended up convincing important sectors of the Chilean left that putting an end to neoliberalism through institutional methods was completely inviable. This powered the idea that the struggle against neoliberalism and the right-wing government needed to be more intense, permanently challenging Piñera's administration through widespread – peaceful and violent – street protests capable of weakening and destabilising the established order as much as possible. In other words, I think that the Chilean left consciously decided to 'bend the rules' by rejecting one of the main rules of the democratic political game that it had abided by until then. In practice, this meant completely stripping the elected government and current Constitution of legitimacy. At the same time, the work of parliamentarians in trying to influence the political process took a back seat and was replaced by social media activism and ongoing protests on the streets.

Allende, Pinochet and the exasperation of the right-left cleavage

During the wave of street protests that followed the October 18th riots, protestors often held placards referring to the past and, in particular, to Salvador Allende and Augusto Pinochet. The former was remembered with nostalgia, linking the October uprising to the Unidad Popular years. For example, one of these placards had a portrait of Allende and said, 'We opened the widest avenues in your honour', referring to Allende's final speech. There were also numerous placards superimposing the faces of Pinochet and Piñera, presenting the latter as a reincarnation of the former dictator. The historical legacy of the 1970–1990 period has undeniably continued to have an important effect on maintaining the right-left cleavage. That is why attention should be paid to this turbulent period in the country's recent political history, providing a greater understanding of the October insurrection and the country's current political scenario.

The widening of the right-left cleavage did not, however, begin with Allende or Pinochet. After Eduardo Frei's victory in 1964, the Chilean right felt that they faced an important threat from Christian Democratic reformism. The land reform, the peasants' unionisation and the empowerment of marginalised urban sectors (the so-called 'promoción popular') were seen by the traditional elite as a serious threat to their interests. That is why the right chose not to support the Christian Democrat candidate Radomiro Tomic in the 1970 presidential elections. Instead, they put their own candidate, former president Jorge Alessandri, up against left-wing candidate, Salvador Allende. The fact that Allende won over the right-wing candidate by such a small margin (36.6 versus 35.3 per cent of the votes) shows the high levels of division and political polarisation Chilean society was experiencing in that period.

The Chilean left also underwent an important radicalisation during the 1960s, influenced by the Cuban revolution and the Che Guevara-inspired guerrilla activity that had emerged in different countries in the region. The local left harshly criticised the reform process backed by Frei, classifying it as a desperate attempt by the local elite to impede the establishment of socialism in Chile. In the Chilean Socialist Party's congress in 1967, it was openly declared that elections were inviable as a way of obtaining political power and that armed struggle was the only way to achieve socialism in Chile. After the defeat of their candidate Salvador Allende in three consecutive presidential contests (1952, 1958, 1964), their hopes of an electoral victory had completely vanished. Therefore, from 1967 onwards, Castroism and Guevarism became the main sources of inspiration and ideological orientation of both this party and of several other Chilean left-wing political organisations (Ortega Martínez, 2008).

Allende eventually won the elections in 1970 against a political right and centre that together made up almost two-thirds of the electorate. The Unidad Popular's government programme established 'ending the domination of the imperialists, monopolies and the landowning oligarchy and starting to construct socialism in Chile' as its main aim (UP, 1969). Although Allende initially tried to keep the reform process within the current legal framework, his government was quickly overcome by pressure from more radical sectors that demanded 'avanzar sin transar' (moving forward without compromising) and accelerating the rhythm of expropriation of rural properties, banks and industries by the state.

The profound political and economic crisis of 1972–1973 led to an important level of radicalisation and polarisation in the heart of Chilean society. On the one hand, adversaries of the Unidad Popular abandoned the idea of trying to put an end to Allende's government by democratic means, quickly adopting an openly Putschist strategy to overthrow it in a violent manner. On the other hand, radicalised left-wing sectors prepared for a 'final' confrontation with the right-wing opposition forces to therefore establish a truly revolutionary government (Roxborough *et al.*, 1977). In those days, there was no place in Chile for those with moderate views and, at that time, very few people supported trying for a political and agreed-upon solution to avoid the collapse of Chilean democracy (Valenzuela, 1978).

The dramatic outcome of the Unidad Popular's political experiment took the right-left cleavage to extraordinary levels. Allende's death and the military regime's violent repression of his followers deeply wounded the hearts and minds of thousands of Chileans. Inspired by a doctrine of national security, the military regime declared an all-out war on left-wing organisations in a frenzied attempt to erase them from the face of the earth forever. At the same time, the use of neoliberal economic policies from 1975 onwards initially caused high levels of unemployment, poverty and social inequality. This generated extreme animosity among working-class sectors for the military regime, as they found themselves defenceless against a state that did not protect them and that only benefited the interests of the most privileged sectors. That is why, from the very start, the military regime was unconditionally supported by and counted on the loyalty of the country's political right and the economic and social elite. These sectors never questioned the systematic violation of human rights or employment exploitation. In addition, the policy of privatising state companies openly favoured the local business elite, leading to the creation of powerful economic-financial conglomerates (Mönckeberg, 2015).

The rage and pain caused by the murders and torture committed and painful exile has forever marked the memories of a whole generation of the Chilean left. Over time, these feelings were passed on to their children and even their grandchildren.[3] After the return to democracy, this hurt was most visibly expressed in demonstrations against the authoritarian period's inheritance – the impunity of those who committed crimes during the dictatorship, the neoliberal model and the 1980 Constitution. In addition, the Chilean left had not forgotten the active role played by the right in the fall of Allende and in the consolidation of Pinochet's regime. That is why they still insist that the military government was a civic-military dictatorship.

By applying the neoliberal economic model from 1975 onwards and due to its auspicious results a few years later, the Chilean right began to leave their initial repressive vindictiveness against left-wing militants behind. As the military regime's consolidation on the economic plane became more and more evident, the right's efforts focused on legally and institutionally consolidating the new authoritarian and neoliberal regime. The approval of the 1980 Constitution was a historical milestone in this sense. Even the defeat of the military regime in the 1988 plebiscite and Patricio Aylwin's triumph in the 1989 presidential elections did not, in practice, pose a direct threat to the continuation of the neoliberal economic model or the 1980 Constitution. After the return to democracy in 1990, the Concertación governments decided not to make any substantial changes to the basis of the dominant economic model. Specifically, they never had the majority they needed in Parliament to either reform or abolish the 1980 Constitution. This meant that the right did not feel threatened by the centre-left governments and so responded positively to the invitation to agree on a 'política de acuerdos' with the Executive to move forward on different economic and social issues. All this was decisive to the increasing depoliticisation and deradicalisation of the majority of right-wing sectors after the return to democracy in 1990.

The important economic boom and the marked reduction in poverty under the Concertación governments visibly contributed to political stability and the search for consensus at a parliamentary level between the centre-left governments and the right-wing opposition. However, the fact that Pinochet remained as Commander-in-Chief of the Army and the impossibility of bringing the people who had violated human rights during the dictatorship to justice were factors that caused permanent tension in the political arena. From 1990 onwards, the radical extra-parliamentary left's battle cry involved bringing those guilty of human rights' violations during the dictatorship to trial under the slogan 'Never forgive, never forget'. Not only did they aim their darts at the military and the political right, but also at the Concertación governments for not having brought those responsible for these crimes to trial.

The Concertación governments adopted a pragmatic stance on the economic model and legislation they had inherited from the authoritarian period, introducing several important tax reforms and a reform to modernise employment legislation (Muñoz, 2007). This meant they could finance ambitious social projects and visibly improve the living conditions of the popular sectors. All these reforms were carried out 'to the extent possible', since the Concertación parties did not have a majority in Parliament. As a result, the Concertación government was forced to negotiate with the right, which did have a comfortable parliamentary representation. This allowed the right to both oversee and put a stop to the Executive's scope of reforms. This control of Parliament and the understanding forged with the Concertación governments meant that the right became more and more relaxed and complacent. This situation encouraged the left's radicalisation. The left was infuriated to see that both the neoliberal economic model and the institutional regime inherited from the dictatorship not only managed to survive but also were apparently consolidated in the new democratic order.

The left-wing moderate-radical cleavage and the triumph of rupturism

One of the most iconic slogans to emerge during the October 18th uprising and its subsequent aftershocks was 'It's not 30 pesos, it's 30 years'. It should be remembered that it was the 30 peso increase in the Santiago underground fare that acted as a catalyst for the October 18th insurrection and the wave of violence that followed in different cities throughout the country. What is so eloquent about this slogan is that it does not criticise the right or the former military dictatorship as one would expect, but rather is aimed to deal a blow to the centre-left Concertación governments. After the return to democracy – and, above all, after the start of the student protests in 2011 – constant criticism of the moderate left has been an ongoing strategy for different sectors of the radical left.

From a historical point of view, the cleavage between the moderate and the radical left increased rapidly after the military coup in 1973. The dramatic end to the 'Chilean road to socialism' created a heated debate within the Chilean left over the causes of the Unidad Popular's government collapse. This discussion was mainly carried out among the exiles spread worldwide and was marked by mutual recriminations from radical and moderate sectors of the Chilean left.

The moderate sector, for its part, underlined the extreme left's important role in the debacle of Allende's government, by radicalising the urban and rural masses and by exacerbating the social conflict in the country to uncontrollable levels. As a result, the extreme left had helped create the sensation that this government posed a great threat to the bourgeoisie, the middle classes and the armed forces, which eventually led to the military coup (Furci, 1984). The extreme left, for its part, explained the military coup mainly as the result of the Unidad Popular's reformist and conciliatory nature. This prevented the masses from having a true and direct participation in how the country was run (the so-called poder popular). According to this interpretation, Allende's government ended up ignoring the revolutionary power of the people, despite the fact that this was the only force capable of permanently crushing the right-wing opposition at the time (Sweezy and Magdoff, 1974).

In the first few years after the coup, the Chilean left referred to the fall of Allende as a *defeat*, implicitly highlighting the purely military nature of the overthrowing of the Unidad Popular government. Over time, however, the Unidad Popular was demystified and secularised and the errors and deficiencies of Allende's government put at the heart of the analysis. A growing number of moderate left-wing political leaders began to talk of the *failure* of the Unidad Popular, highlighting the responsibility of the government coalition itself in this debacle (Garretón, 1987).

In moderate left-wing circles, there was also a critique of the economic policy adopted by Allende's government. The erratic way the economy was run was seen as a determining factor of the profound crisis that emerged from 1972 onwards, seen through hyperinflation and a widespread scarcity of foodstuffs and consumer goods, as well as an enormous public sector deficit (De Vylder, 1976). The second important self-criticism was related to the Unidad Popular's inability to maintain middle-class support and to create a political alliance with the Christian Democrats. In retrospect, it can be concluded that, in order to implement social and economic reforms as radical as those of Allende's government, the support of a broad section of the population was required but never achieved (Bitar, 1979).[4]

The division between the moderate left and the radical left got even worse during exile. While the majority of the moderate left's leaders opted to live out their exile in democratic capitalist countries in Western Europe, the radical left consciously chose destinations like Cuba, the Soviet Union and the communist countries of Eastern Europe (Angell and Carstairs, 1987).

During exile, the moderate Chilean left was strongly influenced by European social-democratic trends and their ability to set up broad government coalitions with centre and even right-wing political forces. Together with the conclusions they had drawn from the Unidad Popular debacle, this experience contributed to a 'process of renovation' within the moderate left (Walker, 1988). This process of ideological and programmatic reformulation culminated in the final break away from Marxism–Leninism and with an unmistakable re-evaluation of democracy that, in the words of Jorge Arrate, needed to turn into 'the space and limit of political action' (Arrate, 1985: 234). This led the moderate left to search out a political alliance with their former adversaries, the Christian Democrats, resulting in the creation of the Democratic Alliance in 1983.

At the other end of the cleavage, radical left sectors described Pinochet's military regime as a fascist one that could only be defeated by an armed rebellion of the people. This emphasis on military action was strengthened after the victory of the Sandinista revolution in Nicaragua in 1979, in which a group of Chileans from this sector took part. Years later, in 1983, the Chilean Communist Party founded the Manuel Rodríguez Patriotic Front (FPMR), a guerrilla organisation whose aim was to defeat Pinochet using armed struggle (Varas *et al.*, 2010).

The fact that the military regime adopted the 1980 Constitution also widened the cleavage between the radical left and the moderate left. For the Communist Party, this proved that Pinochet intended to hold on to power for the rest of his life, which is why the dictatorship had to be attacked by any means possible. Among other things, this led to an attempt to secretly stockpile arms from Cuba and in a frustrated attempt on Pinochet's life in September 1986.

The moderate left, on the other hand, held on to the possibility of defeating Pinochet peacefully through a referendum that, according to the 1980 Constitution itself, was to occur in 1988. In this referendum, Chileans would have the chance to decide 'Yes' or 'No' to prolonging Pinochet's presidency for eight more years. In its temporary rulings, this same Constitution established that, if the 'No' option won, general elections would be held within a year. The referendum held in 1988 made it easier for the democratic forces against Pinochet to unite and organise themselves, joining together in a coalition called the Concertación de Partidos por el No. The historic victory of the 'No' meant that a peaceful transition to democracy was possible, with the process ending in March 1990 with President Patricio Aylwin and his government coalition called the Concertación de Partidos por la Democracia coming to power. From this time forward, the moderate left became a key player in the process of democratic consolidation and in the successful Concertación governments over the next two decades.

The radical left, on the other hand, deliberately removed itself from the history books by choosing a path of armed struggle that completely failed. In addition, it completely stepped away from the democratic forces' successful political-institutional struggle to defeat Pinochet through a referendum. From the restoration of democracy in 1990 up to the student protests in 2006, the Communist Party and other extra-parliamentary left-wing organisations observed with growing helplessness how the Concertación governments continued to exercise hegemony comfortably.

Undoubtedly, the Concertación became the most successful government coalition in the history of Chile (Sehnbruch and Siavelis, 2014). This success was not only reflected in their ability to govern the country for two decades, with the Concertación governments between 1990–2010. This ruling coalition was particularly successful in political, economic and social terms. From a political view, the Concertación governments consolidated a climate of stability and consensus among the country's main political forces. Regarding the economy, during the Concertación, Chile had very good results in terms of economic growth, the expansion of foreign trade, foreign investment and in financial control (low inflation, a public spending surplus, etc.) What is even more important though is that the Concertación governments drastically reduced the country's levels of poverty from almost 40 per cent in 1990 to 12 per cent in 2010.

Although the new democratic authorities eliminated the most controversial traces of neoliberalism in the country, maintaining a free market economy was still a reality that complicated certain left-wing sectors that made up part of the government coalition. Specifically, Pinochet's authorship of the neoliberal system is key to understanding the constant resistance that neoliberalism encountered in the heart of the Concertación's left. This emerged despite the country's good economic and institutional performance since the return to democracy in 1990, which has already been mentioned.

For a long time, 'two souls' coexisted within the Concertación governments. On one hand, there was a social-democratic political sector with its roots in the moderate left and the Christian Democratic Party. This sector was hegemonic within the Concertación governments for the majority of the twenty years that this coalition was in power. It aspired in achieving gradual and moderate changes to the country's political and institutional structures. This sector was given the name in the media of the *autocomplaciente* ('self-satisfying') wing because it was relatively pleased with the Concertación coalition's results in the political, economic and social fields. In practice, this sector tacitly supported the neoliberal economic model and favoured the use of public policies with technocratic leanings to combat social problems. On the other hand, there was also a highly influential left-wing minority within the Concertación that felt extremely uncomfortable with the continuation of neoliberal policies. This was the so-called *autoflagelante* ('self-flagellating') sector, which demanded both that the state take on more of a leading role in economic development and greater levels of citizen participation (Brunner and Moulian, 2002). The struggle between both sectors intensified during Bachelet's first government (2006–2010), to the extent that the different social movements that began to appear on the political scene were openly supported by the Concertación's 'self-flagellating' sector. The struggle between the Concertación's 'two souls' visibly weakened the internal cohesion of Bachelet's first government. In addition, this government was unable to reduce the political volatility of the social movements that regularly took to the streets to protest against the neoliberal model. The 'self-flagellating' sector began to openly attack the powerful group of technocrats in charge of economic policies, led by the Finance Minister, Andrés Velasco. Government technocrats were accused of not paying attention to the demands of civil society when they opposed the exponential increase in public spending demanded by the left on the streets (Silva, 2008).

The right's electoral victory in 2010 put an end to twenty years of Concertación governments. From then onwards, the 'self-flagellating' and anti-neoliberal sectors gained political control within the Concertación conglomerate, which was now the opposition. Free from all the political and ideological limitations that being part of the government had involved up to now, this sector began to distance itself from its social-democratic past and to adopt a more and more radical stance. The emergence of the student movement in 2011 had an important impact on the Concertación, with it coming to identify completely with the anti-neoliberal and rupturist agenda that the young students defended in their recurring street protests. In the end, however, the Concertación parties did not manage to either co-opt the student movement or establish an alliance with their leaders. On the contrary, students and other social movements harshly criticised the Concertación governments and the left-wing parties that were part of this coalition.

Framing the unease and discontent

As has been indicated, the Concertación governments were relatively successful in drawing up and implementing economic and social policies and in their political management of the right-wing opposition. Chile had never before made as much progress as during the Concertación's twenty years in power. Chileans became accustomed to seeing how, year after year, their country had the best social and economic indicators of all Latin America, statistically backed up by the United Nations, CEPAL, the World Bank, the OECD and other international institutions. Also, Chile had reached high levels of governability, political stability and democratic quality, all recognised internationally. Given these successful results, it is almost inconceivable to a foreign observer that a country with these characteristics ended up embroiled in a climate of increasing political unrest and protest against the very governments that made these surprising achievements possible.

Over the last ten years, a series of factors has been mentioned to explain the high level of citizen discontent that, according to some, accounts for the growing wave of anti-system protests. These go from high levels of social inequality to the development of a consumer culture that cannot be completely satisfied and the existence of a political and institutional system that, according to its critics, is agonising. Although many of the factors named are real, in my opinion they do not exclusively explain the radical and violent nature of the majority of street protests after the election of Piñera's government in 2010. Specifically, the majority of these problems also exist – at much more critical levels – in the rest of Latin American countries. Therefore, those behind the theory that blames these factors also need to explain why the majority of Latin America countries have not had to deal with the same level of rebellion as in Chile.

In my opinion, the main reasons why this rebellion took place in Chile and not in other Latin American countries are not to be found in the economic and social spheres, as the majority of studies have tended to indicate. In my opinion, the causes lie first of all in the political arena. In no other Latin American country has the left managed to come to power at the beginning of the 1970s by democratic means but been so abruptly frustrated in their attempt to establish socialism. In no other place was the left defeated in such a violent and traumatic way as in Chile, symbolised by Allende's death. In no other Latin American country did the right manage to defeat the left so convincingly and carry out a successful political, economic, institutional and cultural revolution, maintaining a solid hegemony for more than forty years until the October 18th rebellion. In other words, only Chile had an Allende and a Pinochet, with all the historical, political and emotional weight that they and their political projects have and still hold in collective memory. As opposed to the rest of Latin America, in the experience of the local left, the capitalist system in Chile completely fused with what has come to be called '*the* model'. While in the rest of the region, neoliberalism was attacked from the 1980s onwards in relatively abstract and impersonal terms by the local left, the 'neoliberal model' in Chile had, from the very start, a first name and a surname: Augusto Pinochet. That is why the Chilean left's resistance to and struggle against the 'neoliberal model' – that reached a climax in the October 18th uprising – is so deeply intertwined with the history of the 1970–1990 period and the previously described political cleavages.

Left-wing academic circles played a key role in formulating criticism of the neoliberal model used during the Concertación governments. From the end of the 1990s onwards, there was a discussion about the apparent discontent and unease that had begun to affect Chilean society. The aim was to counter the idea that Chile had turned into a successful country and that the Concertación governments had an excellent performance. Therefore, these scholars produced a series of critical studies in which they criticised several structural aspects of the country's current political and social model. This is particularly the case of the book of sociologist Tomás Moulian published in 1997, called *El Chile actual: anatomía de un mito*. In this book, Moulian harshly criticises the Concertación governments, condemning, among other things, the continuation of the policies implemented by the military regime. This publication had a major impact on public opinion and spent a long time on the bestseller list. The following year, the United Nations Development Programme (UNDP) published its annual report headed by sociologist Norbert Lechner on human development, called *Las paradojas de la modernización*. This report critically analysed what was described as the dark side of the country's modernisation process. It indicated that Chile had turned into a consumer society and that the high levels of materialism were generating distinct levels of disillusionment and discomfort among Chileans.[5] The report contained a series of subjective statements regarding the alleged existence of this discomfort in the country, without offering any definite proof that Chileans were actually experiencing this. José Joaquín Brunner convincingly refuted each of the arguments that appeared in this report. Brunner concludes that neither existing social inequalities, nor government policies, nor the supposed frustration with the democratic transition or the excess of subjective uncertainties can be used to support a theory of unease and discontent (Brunner, 1998: 173–174).

Another important reaction against the thesis of discontent started to position itself in the country's academic and political debate when it appeared in a document called 'La fuerza de nuestras ideas', written in May 1998 by a group of ministers and former collaborators from the liberal wing of the Concertación. It also refuted each of the negative and pessimistic arguments against the traps of Chilean modernity. At the same time, the publication of this document revived a broad controversy within sectors of the Concertación that were more critical of the results of the economic model and who demanded a greater degree of citizen participation. This vision of the Concertación's achievements and mistakes was condensed into the June 1998 document 'La gente tiene razón', written by a long list of Concertación intellectuals and politicians. Both documents brought the struggle within the government conglomeration between 'self-satisfying' and 'self-flagellating' sectors to light.

From 1998 onwards, the works of Moulian, Lechner and other scholars manage to install the idea of Chileans' 'unease and discontent' with the neoliberal economic model permanently. This idea of unease provided a perfect 'framing' for the actions of the parties and movements associated with the radical left against the neoliberal regime in Chile and the Concertación that backed it up.

Nevertheless, the electoral victory of right-wing candidate Sebastián Piñera in 2010 showed that the theory defended by the 'self-flagellating' sector on the existence of a strong level of discontent in Chilean society towards neoliberalism did not totally correspond to reality. If Chileans were so unhappy with neoliberalism, why did the majority vote for Sebastián Piñera, a figure-symbol of local neoliberalism? According to Peña, the emergence of some degree of discontent is natural in countries such as Chile, which had experienced a rapid and profound transformation towards modernity. However, this cannot be automatically interpreted as people's rejection of the neoliberal economic system. According to Peña, Chileans express their discontent with the economic system when the system does not respect their own rules of the game. For example, this has been the case when huge economic conglomerates have conspired to fix prices or when someone has been given a high-powered job based on their connections and not on personal merit (Peña, 2017).

A second powerful 'framing' that resulted fundamental in articulating the resistance to neoliberalism has been provided by the student movement. From 2011 onwards, student organisations began to structure their fight against the Concertación governments around the mobilising concept of 'lucro' (profit). Students started to question, both harshly and successfully, the apparent existence and supremacy of 'profit' in Chilean higher education (Salinas and Fraser, 2012; Mönckeberg, 2013).

The fact that the left-wing student movement did not launch its campaign against Piñera's government from the very first day he became president was simply because of an unexpected event: a strong earthquake and tsunami in Chile on February 27th 2010, only weeks before Bachelet handed over power to the new right-wing president. A state of emergency was declared after this national disaster that left more than 2 million people homeless, meaning that the student movement postponed the actions that it had planned against the new president. The following year, during his annual state of the nation speech on May 21st 2011, Piñera informed the country that the worst of the emergency created by the earthquake was over. Only days later, the student movement started to organise large-scale and often violent protests against for-profit higher education, neoliberalism and Piñera's government. The main party in the radical left – the Communist Party – played a relevant role in mobilising the student movement and in the growing polarisation of the left from then on, although it kept a low profile in public opinion. However, it is relevant that the main leader of the student movement, Camila Vallejos, as well as the leader of the teaching union, Jaime Gallardo, were both members of this party. The main Chilean worker's organisation (CUT) and diverse trade unions that have periodically mobilised against Piñera's government are also controlled by this party (Ponce and Álvarez, 2016).

After becoming part of the Nueva Mayoría government, the Communist party began to exercise an important influence beyond the former Concertación left, both on President Bachelet herself and on the street protests. As well as gaining control of key ministries in the areas of social policies and those aimed at women, the Communist party also deployed an active policy of supporting the student movement protests and social movements in general. The important radicalisation and high levels of intransigence in the Nueva Mayoría government alienated the more moderate sectors of this coalition, particularly in the case of militants from the Christian Democratic party. These felt extremely uncomfortable and powerless when they saw that their party was not taken into account in the decision-making process in Bachelet's second government.

After the Nueva Mayoría government and up to today, the Communist party's influence and presence has continued to increase in the heart of the radical left. After the October 2019 rebellion, its leaders adopted a notable anti-systematic and insurrectional discourse, encouraging the fall of Piñera's government. In addition, the Communist party has managed to expand its political-ideological influence towards the Frente Amplio, with which it established an electoral alliance for the November 2021 presidential elections.

Conclusion

The social uprising that occurred from October 2019 onwards is, in my opinion, closely related to the unprecedented and important process of radicalisation that has occurred at the heart of the Chilean left since 2010. The left's adoption of radical and maximalist views has paradoxically occurred in a society in which the depoliticisation of the majority of the population and relative political stability and economic prosperity have characterised the panorama in the country. As has been indicated in this chapter, what has occurred in Chile has been a process of 'mono-polarisation' by the left, since this phenomenon has not been replicated by the same intensity within the Chilean right. From 2010 onwards, the right has instead taken on a centralist position, similar to that defended by the moderate sectors of the former Concertación.

The marked economic and social progress the country has experienced since the return to democracy in 1990 simply does not provide a sufficient or necessary foundation for the interpretations that identify a series of political-institutional and social problems as the direct causes of the 2019 social uprising. If social inequality, the lack of participation mechanisms, profit, the defencelessness of the middle classes, the collusion between companies and the long list of problems that have been named up to now were really the main causes of October's rebellion, the majority of Latin American countries would also be going up in flames in large scale, experiencing perpetual social uprisings. In my opinion, one of the main reasons why there have not been similar social uprisings in the majority of the Latin American countries is that these countries have not experienced a profound neoliberal revolution like in Chile. The free market regime introduced by Pinochet was, for better or for worse, able to impose a new economic, political, social and cultural order which, with certain modifications, has managed to last for more than four decades. In addition, the Latin American left has not experienced an event as traumatic as the overthrowing of the Unidad Popular government and the abrupt end of the Chilean road to socialism. Finally, the existence of a moderate left with a wide basis of citizen support – as was the case during the Concertación governments in Chile – has not been replicated in the majority of the Latin American countries.

Therefore, in my opinion, the October rebellion can only be understood when it is explored through the lens of history. A study of the important impact of the Unidad Popular government and the military dictatorship on the evolution of the right-left cleavage up until today cannot be overlooked in this analysis. The fact that the Chilean right did not pursue the polarisation and radicalisation processes that occurred in the left is, in my opinion, a show of the hegemony achieved by the neoliberal regime in the country. In fact, the Chilean left's adoption of a rupturist strategy that justified the use of violence was in my view an exasperated response to this reality. In other words, the relative success of the neoliberal system in Chile and its imminent consolidation during the last decade is exactly what led the majority of the Chilean left to follow an openly rupturist strategy within the current political, economic and institutional system. The Nueva Mayoría government clearly failed in its effort to dismantle the country's political, economic and legal-institutional neoliberal structures. This experience led the radicalised left to choose the last option available to them: permanently getting rid of the current political-institutional scenario and trying to overthrow the government and the dominant system through a people's rebellion. In this sense, what occurred in October also marked the final victory of the radical left over a moderate left that today had lost all of its influence on the Chilean political spectrum.

The majority that the radical sectors have gained in the constituent convention may possibly lead to many of the elements of the current Constitution flagged as neoliberal being eliminated. However, those changes on paper will not be able to make great changes to Chilean society, at least not in the short term. What is more likely is that, for quite some time, Chile will continue to be governed by the economic, social and cultural rules that characterise the capitalist modernisation process that began more than four decades ago.

Notes

1 It is suffice to remember that Sebastián Piñera's first government was sometimes called 'the fifth Concertación government'. This is because his administration showed a high degree of continuity with respect to the previous Concertación governments.
2 The Nueva Mayoría government reinstated the image of Salvador Allende. Therefore, during her second government, Bachelet often used large pictures of Allende as a backdrop for her public appearances with phrases such as 'The Chilean people will complete your term'. This heightened the right's suspicions that Bachelet was trying to rebuild a kind of Unidad Popular.
3 After the so-called 'Penguin Revolution' of secondary school pupils that began in 2006, numerous interviews and news reports emerged in which young protesters asserted that they were not only protesting against neoliberalism. But they often said that they were also doing so to honour their parents and grandparents who had suffered with the fall of the Unidad Popular government and been victims of military repression after the coup. In other words, they were trying to turn what their parents and grandparents had been unable to achieve in the past into reality.
4 The lessons learnt from the Unidad Popular debacle were key to the decision taken by the moderate left on the economic and political strategy to use to restore democracy and guarantee future political and economic stability. This made it easier to accept a market model that guaranteed economic growth and financial stability, as well as an alliance with the Christian Democrats to ensure governability and political stability (Boeninger, 1998).
5 The UNDP's annual reports greatly influenced the political agenda of Bachelet's two governments in terms of social inequality, citizen participation and gender equality, as well as in many other areas. During her second government, sociologist Pedro Güell, who for many years was responsible for these reports, became Bachelet's main political adviser.

References

Ampuero, R., J. Black, J. Ramon Valente and G. Varela (2017) *Los 4 (largos) años de la Nueva Mayoría*. Santiago: El Líbero.
Angell, A. and S. Carstairs (1987) 'The Exile Question in Chilean Politics', *Third World Quarterly* 9(1): 148–167.
Arrate, J. (1985) *La fuerza democrática de la idea Socialista*. Barcelona: Ediciones Documentas.
Atría, F., G. Larraín, J.M. Benavente, J. Couso and A. Joignant (2013) *El otro modelo: Del orden neoliberal al régimen de lo público*. Santiago: Debate.
Bitar, S. (1979) *Transición, socialismo y democracia: La experiencia chilena*. Mexico City: Siglo XXI.

Boeninger, E. (1998) *Democracia en Chile: Lecciones para la Gobernabilidad.* Santiago: Editorial Andrés Bello.
Brunner, J.J. (1998) '¿Malestar en la sociedad chilena: ¿De qué, exactamente, estamos hablando?', *Estudios Públicos* 72: 173–198.
Brunner, J.J. (2016) *Nueva Mayoría: Fin de una ilusión.* Santiago: Ediciones B.
Brunner, J.J. and T. Moulian (2002) *Brunner vs Moulian: Izquierda y capitalismo en 12 Rounds.* Santiago: Ediciones El Mostrador.
De Vylder, S. (1976) *Allende's Chile: The Political Economy of the Rise and Fall of the Unidad Popular.* Cambridge: Cambridge University Press.
Furci, C. (1984) *The Chilean Communist Party and the Road to Socialism.* London: Zed Books.
Gárate, M. (2012) *La revolución capitalista de Chile (1973–2003).* Santiago: Ediciones Universidad Alberto Hurtado.
Garretón, M.A. (1987) *Reconstruir la política: Transición y consolidación democrática en Chile.* Santiago: Editorial Andante.
Mayol, A. (2013) *El derrumbe del modelo: La crisis de la economía de mercado en el Chile contemporáneo.* Santiago: LOM.
Mayol, A. and A. Cabrera (2018) *El Frente Amplio en el momento cero: Desde el acontecimiento de 2011 hasta su irrupción electoral en 2017.* Santiago: Catalonia.
Mönckeberg, M.O. (2013) *Con fines de lucro.* Santiago: Editorial Debate.
Mönckeberg, M.O. (2015) *El saqueo de los grupos económicos al Estado chileno.* Santiago: Penguin, Random House.
Muñoz, O. (2007) *El modelo económico de la Concertación 1990–2005: ¿reformas o cambio?* Santiago: Flacso, Catalonia.
Ortega Martínez, L. (2008) 'La radicalización de los socialistas de Chile en la década de 1960', *Revista Universum* 23(2): 152–164.
Peña, C. (2017) *Lo que el dinero sí puede comprar.* Santiago: Taurus.
Pollack, M. (1999) *The New Right in Chile, 1973–97.* London: Palgrave Macmillan.
Ponce, J.I. and R. Álvarez (2016) '¿Comunismo después del fin del comunismo? La política sindical del Partido Comunista de Chile en la postdictadura chilena (1990–2010)', *Nuestra Historia* 1: 100–115.
Roxborough, I. Ph. O'Brien and J. Roddick (1977) *Chile: The State and Revolution.* London: Macmillan.
Salinas, D. and P. Fraser (2012) 'Educational Opportunity and Contentious Politics: The 2011 Chilean Student Movement', *Berkeley Review of Education* 3(1): 17–47.
Sehnbruch, K. and P.M. Siavelis (eds.) (2014) *Democratic Chile: The Politics and Policies of an Historical Coalition, 1990–2010.* Boulder: Lynne Rienner.
Sigmund, P.E. (1977) *The Overthrow of Allende and the Politics of Chile, 1964–1976.* Pittsburgh: The University of Pittsburgh Press.
Silva, P. (2004) 'Doing Politics in a Depoliticised Society: Social Change and Political Deactivation in Chile', *Bulletin of Latin American Research* 23(1): 63–78.
Silva, P. (2008), *In the Name of Reason: Technocrats and Politics in Chile.* University Park: Penn State University Press.
Sweezy, P.M. and H. Magdoff (eds.) (1974) *Revolution and Counter-Revolution in Chile.* New York: Monthly Review Press.

UP (Unidad Popular) (1969) *Programa Básico de Gobierno de la Unidad Popular*. Santiago: Comando de la Unidad Popular.
Valenzuela, A. (1978) *The Breakdown of Democratic Regimes: Chile*. Baltimore: The Johns Hopkins University Press.
Varas, A., A. Riquelme and M. Casals (eds.) (2010) *El Partido Comunista de Chile: Una Historia Presente*. Santiago: Catalonia.
Vergara, P. (1985) *Auge y caída del neoliberalismo en Chile*. Santiago: FLACSO.
Walker, I. (1988) 'Un nuevo socialismo democrático en Chile', *Estudios Cieplan* 24: 5–36.
Walker, I. (2018) *La Nueva Mayoría: Reflexiones sobre una derrota*. Santiago: Catalonia.

3 The rebellion of a disillusioned generation

José Joaquín Brunner

Introduction

The social uprising in October 2019 in Chile, which went on until the beginning of the pandemic in March 2021 and is currently dormant, has been interpreted in several different ways.[1] Only eighteen months after it began, Google Scholar already had 2,830 academic documents mentioning this phenomenon. The attention it has received in the mass media, as well as in conferences, seminars and webinars, has been equally huge, with everyone looking to explain it.

As a result of this incessant inquisitiveness, different narratives about Chilean protests have proliferated, all competing to give significance to the crisis and become part of a greater narrative about the transformation of Chilean society. It is certainly not just an academic topic; the struggle between narratives aims to eventually impose a hegemonic understanding that confers power on those who came up with it. On closer examination, different types of narratives with different scopes compete in the market of ideas, interacting in different ways. This chapter aims to contribute to this discursive exchange with an interpretation based on the reality of what actually happened and guided by a limited set of concepts.

I would like to approach the protest phenomenon from the perspective of the accelerated educational transformation Chilean society has undergone as a result of the widespread growth and universalisation of its higher education (HE). In my opinion, this process has produced an imbalance in the job opportunities, income, recognition and wellbeing provided by society. The uprising was therefore a rebellion against this imbalance, illustrated by the widespread rejection of the aims and cultural means suggested by society in its phase of intense modernisation. This included rejecting the promise of personal and collective success that should have been achieved through effort and investment in HE, leading to social integration and to sharing the benefits of modernity. At a macro-sociological level, in this

DOI: 10.4324/9781003254355-4

effort to interpret and explain the phenomenon, I will refer to my own work on the discontent and contradictions of democratic capitalist modernisation in Chile from 1990 onwards (Brunner, 1998, 2006a, 2006b, 2018). At the same time, on a micro-sociological level, I will turn to secondary information from the very actors the protest represents. Finally, the explanation of this phenomenon will be constructed at an intermediate level, calling on a conceptual model that interprets the social rebellion as a response to collective disillusionment and generational frustration.

The chapter is organised as follows. The first part systematically introduces the organisational, functional and developmental aspects of HE in Chile that serve as a basis for the main argument. Next, I will show how this development was framed within the Chilean elite's discourse on HE's transcendental value for individual wellbeing and economic growth. The third section maintains that HE's ability to expand created an explosion of expectations that led to collective generational disillusionment when they could not be met. The following two sections summarise this generation's experience of entering the job market and the special features of their political socialisation prior to the 2019 uprising. The final part includes two additional sections. One describes and analyses the social basis of the uprising, involving this disillusioned generation. The other offers an explanation of the protest, based on what we have mentioned before. This part understands it as a rebellion of the generation born around 1990, which is facing an imbalance between the cultural aim of integration into capitalist modernity and the failure of HE qualifications to ensure that this promise is fulfilled.

Higher education: streamlined facts

For the purposes of this analysis, it is interesting to highlight four aspects of HE's outward features. Firstly, there has been a rapid growth in student numbers, increasing almost five times between 1990 and 2019. As a result, over the space of three decades, Chile has gone from an initial phase of restricted HE access to an intermediate one involving large-scale access. In addition, from 2007 onwards, the country entered a phase of extremely rapid growth, which took the gross participation rate up to 91 per cent in 2019. Therefore, at the time of the uprising, Chile had an HE rate that was 17 per cent higher than the OECD average and 38 per cent higher than the Latin American one. This has led to a dramatic intergenerational jump in education. While, in the parents' generation (54–65 years old), only 16 per cent had gone on to HE, this percentage rose to 34 per cent among the children's generation (25–34 years old).

Secondly, the opening up of access to HE has reflected an increase in the participation of young people from all of society's socioeconomic levels. In other words, it included those from the 20 per cent of homes with the lowest incomes, whose attendance went up from 4.4 per cent in 1990 to 37.6 per cent in 2017. This intense intergenerational mobility and the widening of the social pool for student recruitment resulted in greater socioeconomic and cultural diversity among the student population. In addition, it has directly impacted the 'inherited effect', which has progressively decreased. In effect, students from families where one of the members has already attended HE went down to barely 30 per cent, while first-generation HE students in the family increased to 70 per cent.

Thirdly, as the number of students has increased, the number of graduates (either from universities or from technical colleges) has also gone up. In the three decades prior to 2019, these numbers went up ten and six times, respectively, from 14,900 to 240,000 in total. When the Chilean population was asked in 2017 about the most important reason to go on to university or technical college, their answers pointed towards financial reward and social mobility on one hand and personal and vocational development on the other. Hoping to improve their income and job opportunities was the response of 41 per cent, while 24 per cent referred to personal development and 15 per cent to having a better life than their parents. Finally, 12 per cent indicated that they wanted to follow their vocation or get ready to work in a particular area, 4 per cent wanted to be more valued socially and 3 per cent to learn. Asked on the same occasion about whether they agreed that a young person who had gone on to HE 'would have more chances of having a better life than their parents', 81 per cent said yes.[2]

Given the huge influx of students going on to HE, however, it is worth bearing in mind a few important considerations. Students going on to HE have a prior cognitive-scholarly performance that is unequal, conditioned by their socio-familial origins, early socialisation in the home, early education and school trajectory, as well as other factors involving context and personal characteristics. Going to university itself involves an additional filter, consisting of an entrance test whose results match the applicants' socio-familiar origins. As a result, students are grouped selectively; those with the highest scores in the university entrance test – usually from the highest echelons of the socioeconomic and cultural scale – choose and are accepted by high-quality universities whose quality is measured on how long they have been established (Cociña et al., 2017: 97). The other students are distributed between universities and other types of institution with little to no socio-academic selectivity. This confirms well-known hypotheses such as that of maximally maintained inequality (MMI) and essentially maintained inequality (EMI), in which educational inequalities tend to persist despite HE's growth. This is because young people from the upper social classes are always in a better position to take advantage of the new opportunities created by this expansion (MMI) or to access opportunities of a better quality (EMI) (Boliver, 2011).

This means that very different educational trajectories now exist for young people from different socioeconomic strata. This calls into question HE's meritocratic nature and reveals that, despite study opportunities' widespread growth, these are still tied to the socioeconomic conditions of the homes students come from.

In the same way, once young people from the same age range graduate HE and enter the job market, their average wages differ and are segmented depending on the HE institute they went to. The wages offered to graduates from shorter programmes resulting in diplomas are only slightly higher than the income of those who have completed secondary school, with no significant differences according to their family's socioeconomic conditions. For technical college graduates, the difference in social strata is also only moderate, although it is more pronounced for graduates from secondary school. Finally, in the case of university graduates, wages are clearly higher, depending on both the kind of institution they graduate from and their family's socioeconomic strata (Cociña et al., 2017: 314).

In all, over the last thirty years and especially from the second half of the 2010s, the study opportunities available at an HE level in Chile have broadened significantly. It is understood that the road to getting an HE qualification is relatively meritocratic and that it serves as a passport to careers with better wages and greater social recognition. However, in practice, this huge outpouring of wishes, efforts and expectations has not altered the underlying hierarchy of social positions and has instead led to an explosive multiplication of graduates but an unaltered connection between origins and destinies.

Perception and value of higher education in the elite's discourse

HE was assigned great importance in the agenda and discourse of the Chilean elite behind the transition to democracy. The same happened with the programmes and public policies of the governments of the time and with the transformations experienced by Chilean society during the three decades prior to the 2019 uprising. HE was a strategic discursive basis for both democratic reconstruction and the country's socioeconomic modernisation. Therefore, a cultural discourse flourished, centred on individual effort and merit, intergenerational mobility and participation in the benefits of modernity.

Cultivated by the elite throughout the political and ideological spectrum, this led to education being valued in multiple different ways. It was a key lever for economic growth (human capital, job productivity, family income, competition between companies and the integration of the Chilean economy into global markets). It was also a determining factor for social mobility (within and between generations, to overcome poverty, to become middle class through personal effort and to obtain material belongings in a developed society). Finally, education was also presented as the main means of acquiring and developing the abilities needed to be part of a contemporary culture (based on technical scientific knowledge, individual autonomy, freedom of choice and entrepreneurship).

This discourse, which transformed education on the basis of personal emancipation and the wealth of nations, was supported and also motivated by the choir of voices that emerged every day to support it from within the most influential international bodies (the OECD, the World Bank and, at a regional level, ECLAC-UNESCO (1992) and the IDB). This has been captured in a range of documents, from the Jomtien World Declaration on 'Education for All' in 1990 to the Incheon Declaration in 2015. Equally, business discourse worldwide pointed in this direction and served as a basis for international comparisons, as well as for rankings of human capital, the command of basic abilities and twentieth-century employability. From the 1990s onwards, there was an important emphasis on education and its key role as a lever for nations' development, although with less conviction and unanimity than at the beginning.

Inflated expectations and collective disillusionment

This intensely affirmative discourse permeated the conscience of every sector of Chilean society.[3] Even more importantly, it shaped the expectations of a lower-class generation born into democracy around 1990. A survey in 2000 showed that people did not name 'abuse or injustice in the system', 'having had poor parents', 'a lack of generosity from those who have more', 'bad luck' or 'the government's bad economic policies' to justify why they were poor. Quite the opposite, these were the reasons mentioned the least, accounting for barely more than 15 per cent of the answers. Conversely, those belonging to the lower classes complained a lot about 'a lack of education', with 40 per cent identifying this as the main explanation for their poverty. Education also appears as an increasingly important factor to explain other people's economic success (CEP survey, March–April 2000). This positive opinion about the power of education has lasted over time. For example, a 2017 survey indicated that a large part of the Chilean population aged over 18 (between 71 per cent and 81 per cent) 'agreed' or 'very much agreed' with the statement that a young person who has gone on to HE would have more chances of finding work, being valued by society, earning an income, gaining knowledge and abilities and having a better life than their parents (CEP survey, July–August 2017). A previous survey in 2015 by the same body registered what people believed about key or very important aspects for getting ahead in life. In first place, with more than 50 per cent each, were 'a good level of education' (63 per cent), 'hard work' (57 per cent) and 'being ambitious' (51 per cent). These beat out other aspects such as 'meeting the right people', 'having parents with a high level of education', 'coming from a rich or well-off family', 'a person's race or ethnicity', 'a person's sex', 'being a man or a woman', 'the person's religion' and 'paying bribes' (CEP survey, November 2015).

In a scenario in which HE's value was being collectively exalted, it is not surprising that, in 2019, when only 24 per cent of the population aged between 25 and 64 years had gone on to HE, around 90 per cent of secondary school pupils at 15 hoped to go on to HE too. This number is far above OECD countries' average, which is no higher than 50 per cent (OECD, 2019). Even more noteworthy is the fact that 70 per cent of Chilean students in 2006 thought that they would work as a manager, public or private executive or as a professional with relative job autonomy, such as a lawyer, engineer or doctor (OECD, 2006) in the future, compared to the OECD average of 55 per cent. In other words, they expected an income and status equal to society's most prestigious and well-paid positions that, even in HE systems accessible to minorities, are exclusively reserved for young heirs from families with more economic, social, academic and cultural capital (Bourdieu and Passeron, 2009). In a system like the Chilean one, with universal large-scale access, this promise was far from being fulfilled and, in fact, was never destined to occur. As Bourdieu indicates in another piece, newcomers to education 'are led, by the mere fact of having access to it, to expect it to give them what it gave others at a time when they themselves were still excluded from it' (Bourdieu, 1984: 143).

We are therefore faced with a situation involving high aspirations, which is continually nurtured by the official discourse that promises that the cultural goals of society can be met through HE. This pushes young people from the lower classes to invest heavily – effort, discipline, time and resources – in the rules of the game on offer. However, as we saw earlier, it could be said that the system only fulfils HE's entry-level promise and, even then, only offers a combination of opportunities distributed in a hierarchal way through a descending cascade of possibilities to reach the goal.

It is worth mentioning a series of other obstacles to fulfilling the vested promise of education, such as students' socio-familiar background, the schools they have attended and the effectiveness of institutions in the educational system. Firstly, between a third and a quarter of Chilean students enrolled in HE (depending on the type and level of institution) drop out either during or at the end of their first year. Secondly, the timely completion rate of a cohort of Chilean students on shorter courses is 23 per cent, increasing to 46 per cent when an additional three years of study are added. At a degree level, the numbers are 16 per cent and 51 per cent respectively, well under the OECD average (of 40 per cent and 69 per cent, respectively) using comparable information from 23 countries (OECD, 2019). Thirdly, the graduation rate by socioeconomic level is highly unequal; according to the income quintiles from richest to poorest, the percentage of graduates is 49 per cent, 19 per cent, 10 per cent, 6 per cent and 4 per cent, respectively (Carrillo *et al.*, 2018). Fourthly, the number of people who have gone on to HE that are underemployed based on their abilities or qualifications (implying an insufficient use of workers' job skills) increased from around 400,000 people mid-2009 to around 700,000 at the time of the social uprising (Bravo, 2020, 2021). Fifthly, a significant number of HE graduates – around a million between 2006 and 2020, including those who have dropped out – financed their studies with a state-guaranteed loan. Paying off this loan holds an important place in the experiences and discourse of the disillusioned generation. Sixthly and lastly, in an important number of university careers, graduates' gross monthly income the first and fifth year after entering the job market was barely 1.3 and twice the minimum monthly income, respectively,[4] for workers aged between 26 and 65 years.

The structural imbalance between having aspirations and actually materialising them – in other words, between what the educational system promises and how fulfilling these promises is limited, or rather between the *illusion*[5] of the game that must be played and the limited financial and social gains offered by the job market – have led to what Bourdieu (1984: 144) calls 'collective disillusionment'. He analyses this particular imbalance by calling it the 'hysteresis effect' (Bourdieu, 1990: 62). This indicates that the aspirations and expectations created at a certain time can have completely different results when they materialise later on and when the conditions in which they were initially conceived no longer exist. Therefore, at the beginning, when expectations were only valid for a privileged minority, HE qualifications commanded high wages and were a status symbol. This is in great contrast with what occurred afterwards, when these qualifications become more widespread and therefore lost their social and market value. This same phenomenon is also known as credential inflation (Collins, 1979) or credentialism (Chiroleu and Marquina, 2017) and can lead to collective outbursts of frustration towards or rebellion against the system, as we will see later on.

Experiences of a disillusioned generation in the job market

Given the fact that, in Chile, a group of young people were the first in their families to go on to HE and to experience the 'hysteresis effect' that Bourdieu talks about, there has also been an increasing number of young adults from 2010 onwards becoming 'first generation professionals', as described in literature. These usually come from the two or three lowest-quintile homes and the majority go on to HE universities or institutions that are only moderately selective, only slightly selective or not selective at all (open to all). As a study indicates, 'first-generation professionals . . . have demonstrated through their careers that they are capable of mobilising all their resources: time, years without income, money, acquisition of debt, among others, based on getting a university degree and becoming professionals' (Ramos Matus, 2018: 90).

As we saw before, a large group of around 250,000 young professionals and specialists enter the job market in Chile each year. They experience their first dis-*illusio* when having to prove the functional value of the qualification they were granted by their educational institute. As a young physiotherapist from the disillusioned generation indicated:

> you realise that having a degree, a certificate in your hand, you say, oh, you know, I'm a professional, but it doesn't mean anything, it's not a guarantee that all your dreams will come true, that all your ideas will come to fruition.
>
> (Ramos Matus, 2018: 81)

This quote clearly shows the conflict between dreams and reality, between the imagined job market and its current state and between the prestige promised by or attributed to the institution granting the degree and the actual prestige their qualifications have in the working world. In short, there is a gulf between anticipated status and income and what is actually recognised in society. A law graduate from a private regional university indicates that

> nowadays, professionals are churned out and churned out and churned out and there are a lot of learned but unemployed people; people with great university degrees, lots of studies, but who can't find work; they're working in sales or whatever just to survive, because in the end what you need is money to live.
>
> (Vásquez Palma, 2017: 189)

Told here in their own words, the encounter of this first generation of professionals with the job market therefore shows the difficulty of getting a job, since degrees from relatively new HE institutions – that are not selective or lack a good reputation – are not recognised. In addition, it is likely that the members of this generation did not have social media providing information, contacts and patronage (social capital) when they entered the job market, nor did they have employability capital from a recognised institution. It is also possible that they are discriminated against because of their family background, prior schooling and lack of the cultural capital traditionally associated with professional positions. It is also likely that they have trouble finding jobs consistent with the area of knowledge they studied (field of study sub-employment).

Literature has also detected a set of frustrations and affronts associated with this first generation's HE once these professionals actually find work. For example, they find it difficult to gain recognition in the workplace from their peers from more prestigious universities. There is also a perception of inconsistencies among the status of different colleagues, specifically related to those high up in office. They also receive little consideration for personal merit and effort during their career, compared to peers with different social origins and client, political and friendly networks. They experience high rotation in jobs frequently done without formal contracts; they come to form part of the so-called 'boletariado' (freelancers). In the same way, the knowledge that they have acquired is devalued, which leads to feelings of de-professionalisation or uncertainty among those who, within a certain profession, receive the lowest incomes and the least recognition. Additionally, there is a perception of professional discontinuity, due to frequent employment migration towards the service sector (e.g. call centres), sales (e.g. supermarkets) or entrepreneurship (e.g. being self-employed for a distribution or transport platform) to earn an income that their profession in itself cannot guarantee them. Finally, they have feelings of anguish and uncertainty due to their low income, debt and the lack of a timeframe to consolidate the new status promised by HE.

As the study of Jara Villarroel summarises, the greatest problem with this sample of first-generation professionals is 'their lack of job stability and the low wages they receive for the work they do, leading to an uncertainty as far as their everyday material progress that grows given the privatisation of social services' (2020: 92).

Political socialisation of a disillusioned generation

We will now locate the disillusioned generation on a timeline to see how their political socialisation – the education of attitudes, values, behaviour and orientation in the political sphere – has occurred over the last thirty years (Neundorf and Smets, 2017). These people were born around the years when the transition from Pinochet's dictatorship to democracy began, between the years 1985 and 1990 and the majority were born into poverty. We should remember that, in 1990, almost 40 per cent of the Chilean population lived in poverty. At a time when access to HE was reserved for a minority, most of their parents had dropped out of secondary school. For example, in 1990, the gross rate of participation in HE was around 20 per cent, with around 20,000 students graduating from university or technical college.

Those born around 1985 started primary school in 1991 and finished it eight years later in 1997. They went on to secondary school the following year and finished their twelve-year cycle of compulsory education in 2002. They entered HE the following year, with the first of them graduating around 2005/2006 or in 2007/2009 for longer degree courses. Therefore, by the 2010s, there was already a constant flow of adults from this generation entering the job market, with high expectations and aspirations (the *illusio* of the educational game). The majority – and especially first-generation professionals – experienced the 'hysteresis effect' and subsequent disappointment, as seen in the previous section. This generation's political socialisation therefore occurred right in the middle of the transition to democracy, in homes that would soon become part of the country's greatest modernisation and economic growth transformation of the twentieth- and twenty-first centuries.

On the other hand, politics unfolds through institutional channels and as an intense and continuous inter-elite negotiation. This occurs when society is going through a massive expansion of opportunities and benefits, in a cultural climate characterised and sometimes even exaggerated by the dual promise of sustained material progress and continuous social mobility. Undoubtedly, this climate permeated the early socialisation of the 'children of the democracy', an issue that has been studied very little up to now.

A reasonable hypothesis is that this disillusioned generation received its most intense political socialisation not at home or even at school, but rather in the cultural environment of the student movement and its struggles. The first of the three decades being analysed was the one most intensely dedicated to the transition to and installation of democracy, the gradual deconstruction of the authoritarian regime and the modernisation of the economy and society. During this time, young students were practically absent from the public eye. The student movement slowly began to reconfigure itself at university campuses, with two timid initial concessions granted: the internal democratisation of university power to get rid of the authoritarian legacy and a return to state universities being free and private ones being directly subsidised by the state.

In the second decade post-dictatorship, beginning in 2001, a protest was held that was led by secondary school pupils, who took to the streets to demand free transport, a free university admissions test and a reduction in the length of the full school day implemented in 1997. This protest was one of the first signs of an anti-privatisation and pro-equity agenda that the student movement would later successfully pick up on.

The main milestone of this decade, however, was the 'Penguin Revolution' in 2006, led by secondary school pupils countrywide, like the previous event described. It gained widespread support from the public and had important political effects. On May 30th that year, around a million pupils from all year groups, accompanied by their parents or legal guardians, protested on the streets against school education whose cost was shared with families. The key elements they demanded of the school system were the following: (i) the end of the Organic Education Law (LOCE), approved the last day of Pinochet's dictatorship (on March 10th 1990); (ii) the end of the 'neoliberal model' of education, which they indicated was sustained on the pillars of privatisation, vouchers, cost-sharing, profit and social segregation and (iii) action to improve state-school education run by town councils, which had effectively been abandoned by the government.

Given the massive support the protest received, President Bachelet's recently elected government (2006–2010) convened a Presidential Commission for the Quality of Education, made up of 81 members representing the educational community and different social, political and cultural forces. After deliberating, the commission issued a majority report that proposed abolishing the LOCE, recognising the right to free, obligatory quality education, reorganising schools' run by town councils and a series of other changes to ensure greater equity and quality in learning opportunities. Over the following three years, in the midst of sporadic protests on the streets, the government drew up and sent the new General Education Law N° 20,370 (for schools) to Congress, which was passed in December 2009. This defined a new kind of institutionality and governance for the school system and incorporated some of the petitions of the 'Penguin Revolution'. However, it did not change the system's political-economical basis or the mixed provision regime, although it did stipulate that private administrators had to set themselves up as not-for-profit companies with a single line of business.

The third decade, which covers the most recent period of the political socialisation of the disillusioned generation, involved two other milestones before ending in the social uprising in October 2019. Both reflect decisive moments in the HE-based student protests.

The first, in 2011, called into question the basis of the HE system, which had not been updated by the General Education Law, remaining essentially untouched, therefore, since the LOCE. The student movement's demands were aimed at resolving 'unequal access to quality education, segregation, the dismantling of public education, fraud and families going into excessive debt', as one of the protest's leaders remembers. He adds that 'what set off the protests that year was the fact that people became aware that the inequalities in Chile were ongoing, that segregation was something constant and that "meritocracy" was a fairy tale sold to the majority of Chileans'.[6] For the first time, this movement gained widespread support countrywide from students from all kinds of HE institutions, both state and privately run. It lasted for six months with 36 protests, several involving around 100,000 students in Santiago and a march that brought together a million people in August of that year. In addition, the movement widened and diversified its repertoire of protesting to include occupations, strikes, hunger strikes, the widespread banging of pots and pans in the evenings, marches, choreography and street performances (Reyes and Vallejo, 2013). It also provided an opportunity for a new generation of student leaders, including a group of university students who, as secondary school pupils, had taken part in the 'Penguin Revolution'.

Similar to that 'revolution' and now to an even greater extent, the 2011 demonstrations were based on an ideological agenda that both questioned and broke away from the HE 'neoliberal model'. It demanded structural changes, greater state control of the system, the reinforcement of public state education, the exclusion of for-profit institutions and free education. Considered the most important and significant milestone in the history of student protests in three decades, the 2011 movement lost its momentum towards the end of the school year (December), in the midst of arguments among its leaders about how to negotiate with the government and the annual renovation of student leadership. Its repercussions were still being felt in 2012 and 2013 though, but there were fewer protests. Several of their demands did though inspire the HE reform programme of President Bachelet's second government (2014–2018). In effect, during this administration, the HE legal framework inherited from the dictatorship was finally abolished, with a new Higher Education Law (N° 21,051) approved in May 2018.

The disillusioned generation's political learning curve ended with the so-called 'Feminist May' in 2018. Involving female students and university academics reacting to gender violence, it proposed an agenda that rebuked gender discrimination in female student access to HE institutions and degree courses, denouncing any kind of violence or sexual harassment. In addition, it called out the gaps in equality between men and women in academic degree courses and in holding positions at the head of institutions. It also rejected androcentricity in the production of knowledge. At the same time, these demands were adopted by a student movement that demanded free, quality and non-sexist HE. In addition, this student movement set new standards for a language and behaviour that recognised gender equality and condemned any 'symbolic violence' carried out under the protection of a patriarchal culture.

On May 16th 2018, a women's march was convened in Santiago, bringing together more than 100,000 people. An article written about that day indicated that the protests staged in the city were

> provocative, using symbolic content directed at society as a whole, with actions that demonstrated their capacity to organise themselves,

strength and enthusiasm: women covering their faces, naked torsos, ponytails, covered mouths, containing messages against the social and symbolic order of masculine domination.

(Ubilla et al., 2019: 228)

This same piece shows that this feminist display led to universities beginning institutional investigations and sanctioning harassment and gender violence. They also drew up behaviour and gender equality recognition protocols as part of their institutional regulations and actively promoted a series of female academic networks with, for example, feminist lawyers, political experts, psychologists and scientists, aimed at refocusing their research and teaching.

The social basis for the October 2019 protest

An opinion poll of demonstrators during the month of November 2019 in Santiago de Chile (NUDESOC, 2020), just weeks after the social uprising, showed that they had a distinct age-related generational profile and that the majority had gone on to HE. Carried out directly on the streets in the centre of Santiago between November 8th and 29th 2019 on a sample of demonstrators over 18, the survey revealed that their average age was 33.[7] In other words, the protesters fit right in the middle of our timeline. There were similar number of women and men, with the majority (49 per cent) living in the neighbourhoods of Santiago Centro, Ñuñoa, Puente Alto, Maipú, La Florida and Providencia. In other words, the protesters came from neighbourhoods characterised by having a lower class that was not poor, a lower middle class, an intermediate middle class and a reduced segment from the upper middle class. Making up more than half the sample, protesters had completed HE (32 per cent university HE, 13 per cent technical college HE and 10 per cent HE post-graduate studies) and 9 per cent had dropped out. The rest of those taking part in the protests had finished secondary school (32 per cent) and only 3 per cent had less education than that.

Even if there is a possible bias favouring people with HE, their high number in the sample is still noteworthy, especially when compared to their prevalence in the population aged between 25 and 34 years, equal in 2019 to 34 per cent. In addition, 54 per cent of the protesters indicated that they were the breadwinner in their household; 64 per cent identified as left-wing, 15 per cent with the centre, 1 per cent with the right-wing, 18 per cent said they had no political leanings and 2 per cent did not know or did not respond. It stands out that a high number of demonstrators (93 per cent) were 'very dissatisfied with' or 'dissatisfied' with democracy, while only 6 per cent were 'satisfied' or 'very satisfied'. The three main demands mentioned by the protesters were pensions (75 per cent), health (58 per cent) and education (57 per cent), followed by social justice (23 per cent), a new Constitution (21 per cent), employment and decent wages (16 per cent) and human rights and no more impunity (10 per cent). A total of 47 per cent said they had taken to the streets 'often' or 'very often' over the last ten years, 43 per cent 'sometimes' or 'rarely' and 9 per cent 'never before' (NUDESOC, 2020).

On one hand, another national survey carried out between November 28th 2019 and January 6th 2020 on people aged over 18 years throughout the country showed majority approval for the protests in general terms. Of those surveyed, 55 per cent approved, 11 per cent did not approve, 10 per cent initially supported them and then opposed them, 7 per cent rejected them initially and then supported them, 15 per cent neither backed nor rejected them and 2 per cent did not know or did not answer. Those surveyed thought that the main reasons for the demonstrations were inequality (38 per cent), low pensions (16 per cent), high cost of living (16 per cent) and low quality of public education and healthcare (13 per cent) (CEP survey, December 2019).

Finally, another survey carried out between January 6th and 15th 2020 over 18 years of age of both sexes revealed that 79 per cent agreed with the protests and 60 per cent thought that there had been no response to the uprising's social demands up to then. People's self-identification with a social class seems to have changed after the protest: 56 per cent said they belonged to the lower class, 39 per cent to the middle class and 5 per cent to the upper class (MORI-FIEL, 2020). Three years prior to the uprising, however, 19 per cent identified as lower class, 66 per cent as middle class and 16 per cent as upper class (Cociña *et al.*, 2017: 164). This shows a significant U-turn in the subjective perception of class within the Chilean population.

In summary, the social uprising in the last three months of 2019 in Chile was mainly supported by a large generation of young adults aged between 30 and 40 years, with HE qualifications or at least incomplete post-secondary education. This generation's political socialisation occurred in conjunction with the country's democratisation process at the end of the Pinochet dictatorship. In their youth, they developed extremely high educational, employment and social mobility expectations, driven by a huge expansion of the skills and opportunities associated with the modernisation of both the economy and society.

This chapter argues that despite their enthusiasm for protesting – as seen in the first two decades of the twentieth century – secondary school and HE students and the feminist movement also discovered that widespread access to education did not lead to either the desired or the imagined benefits. Their social conscience was forged during the protests on the streets and through social media, on the margin of politics. They came to identify with the left, more because of their elective relationship with this sector than a commitment to its organisations and ideological ideas. This radicalised their anti-system perceptions and opinions on entering the job market, with members of this generation suddenly facing a different reality to the high aspirations of recognition cultivated from early on. They were

> candidates for engineers, doctors, nurses, but withdrawn in choice, faced with the difficulties they experience when trying to be what they aspired to be with those attributes. It's not a matter of declining . . . it's more the confrontation of a promise that moves them, takes them away from, that does not meet the terms agreed on at the beginning of the journey.
>
> (Canales *et al.*, 2020: 95)

This disillusioned generation therefore came to include the up-and-coming middle classes working temporary jobs, similar and closer to a lower class that is not poor and the lower middle class, but with (either complete or incomplete) HE acquired according to the rules of the game (that *illusio*), only to discover in the end that this promise was not going to be met. Their income is low and appears even more diminished when compared to their expectations. Already in possession of qualifications, they have discovered that these do not guarantee them any of the imagined basic assurances previously associated with educational status (social security, healthcare, housing and a good education for their children). Their new status in society is therefore ambiguous. They have found themselves

> on a fragile rung of the system of opportunities in Chilean society. They are a low elite as described by the quoted study: passed over for managerial positions – since they have a competitive disadvantage compared to those from higher classes – and over-educated for middle-management positions or ones that require few qualifications which is where they usually end up.
>
> (Canales *et al.*, 2020: 99)

In summary, they are a disillusioned generation.

Protests as a way of rebelling against anomie

This generation's disillusionment is, to a certain extent, similar to the phenomenon noted by sociologist James Coleman in societies whose development and modernisation processes began in the mid-1960s (Coleman, 1965). Imbalances occurred between rapidly expanding education for secondary school pupils and a slower growing economy and job market, creating what he called 'the anomic potential of unemployed school leavers' and a 'vast and nearly uncontrollable increase in the number of unemployed and underemployed school leavers' (Coleman, 1965: 27, 29). In addition, he maintained that this more educated generation had been left behind by the previous one, since the benefits obtained from their qualifications no longer guaranteed the same level of income or status.

Another classic academic contribution from the same time and with a similar theoretical approach highlights the fact that 'the incorporation of substantial elements of the population into the middle classes has escalated their expectations and aspirations, thereby causing a more intense reaction if these are not met in reality' (Crozier *et al.*, 1975: 158). Similarly, neither the 'bourgeois' nor 'conservative sociology' is numb to the transformations that societies experience as a result of rapid modernisation. In fact, this leads to a hypothesis that suggests that, as a group's living conditions improve, their wishes also grow. 'These grow quicker than they improve and can result in dissatisfaction and rebellion' (Geschwender, 1964: 249).

Using a different approach to those previously mentioned but agreeing with their conclusions, Pierre Bourdieu observes that the widespread increase in educational qualifications can eventually work against their very aim. In a section titled 'A Disillusioned Generation' in his book *Distinction*, this author refers specifically to the structural imbalance between aspirations and the educational system's results during a stage of rapid spread and qualification inflation, when job opportunities no longer guarantee the return on human capital expected. He says that 'the collective disillusionment which results from the structural mismatch between aspirations and real possibilities is the source of the disaffection towards work, that refusal of social finitude, which generates all the refusals and negations of the adolescent counter culture' (Bourdieu, 1984: 144).

Referring to the 1968 generation of rebellious young French people, he concludes that the previously mentioned 'hysteresis effect' was at the root of their rioting. In other words, there was a sharp imbalance between aspirations and satisfaction, given the fact that these emerged in a different context and lost value as they became more widespread, leading to feelings of being defrauded. He talks of a 'misled and disillusioned generation' because, like Chile, the promise education made was not met and students faced a reality that, rather being recognised, was denied. He argues that

> the structural de-skilling of a whole generation, who are bound to get less out of their qualifications than the previous generation would have obtained, engenders a sort of collective disillusionment: a whole generation, finding it has been taken for a ride, is inclined to extend to all

institutions the mixture of revolt and resentment it feels towards the educational system.

(Bourdieu, 1984: 144)

How can this be explained? I suggest using the theory of anomie as described by Merton (1969), which incorporates and completes the previous analyses and provides an explanation for the Chilean protests in October 2019.

In two publications revised over the space of four decades, Merton explores the topic of anomie, which he says is understood as the discouragement, deinstitutionalisation or disorientation felt by different groups or classes in society that have been created structurally. These are expressed as an imbalance between cultural goals (CG) and the institutional means (IM) to achieve them. As has been seen up to now in the case of Chile, this imbalance has been produced between the new middle class's cultural goal of achieving status, material belongings and symbolic recognition and the means required to reach them, consistent with getting HE qualifications. This promise has been broken, initially due to Bourdieu's 'hysteresis effect', which leads to 'previously appropriate categories of perception and appreciation being applied to a new state of the qualification market', an effect that 'is proportionately greater for agents who are more remote from the educational system and who are poorly or only vaguely informed about the market in educational qualifications' (Bourdieu, 1984: 142).

From a human capital theory approach, a phenomenon therefore arises that is usually described as involving education or the inflation and devaluation of educational degrees, resulting in a lower (and sometimes even negative) rate of private return on the investment made. Moreover, according to this approach, this is a short-term phenomenon that is then automatically adjusted to the very dynamic of the job market's offer and demand. In this case, then, the impact of being 'overeducated' is individual and psychological (job dissatisfaction), although in larger-scale and longer-lasting situations it can also cause social and political effects, as Burris (1983) foresaw in his seminal paper.

This chapter, however, deals with the social impact and ideological and political scope of this imbalance, which has a structural nature and results in states of anomie. Merton indicates that this imbalance can manifest itself in different ways among groups throughout society's stratification. He also distinguishes five different ways of adapting to anomie, depending on how individuals react to a disjunction of goals and means.

Using his own terminology, conformity emerges when goals and means are accepted, which normally occurs in a social order with a certain equilibrium (+CG/+IM). On the other hand, separation occurs when goals and means are rejected, leading some individuals or groups to take refuge in a world with its own rules. This is seen in certain communities and sects that have separated from the usual social traffic in order to cultivate a different way of life, without socially accepted goals and means (-CG/-IM). Maintaining cultural goals through new legitimate means leads to an adaptive method that Merton calls innovation (+CG/-IM). For example, this is something that occurs when certain individuals, in order to achieve the goal of dominant cultural integration, substitute the well-known means (HE qualifications) for a shortcut such as a successful commercial business venture. On the other hand, giving up on the goal – but with an apparent unfounded insistence on the means – leads to ritualism that, in our scenario, involves people who insist on continuing accumulating qualifications despite being in a career saturated with people with degrees and in which over-education has become structural (-CG/+IM).

As well as the previously mentioned individual or small group adaptation methods – whether these are conformist, separatist, innovative or ritualistic – Merton adds a fifth one he calls rebellion. Together with rejecting the accepted goals and means (-CG/-IM), this aims to substitute them actively and energetically for another vision and type of order in society. As Deflem and Triplett indicate, 'rebellion stands apart from the other deviant modes of adaptation by its deliberate attempt to challenge the existing cultural structure' (Deflem and Triplett, 2018: 146). This is exactly what can be seen in Chile.

Conclusion

The analysis presented in this chapter and the conceptual devices proposed – from Coleman to Bourdieu and Merton – lead me to conclude that a disillusioned generation is at the root of the protests that began in Chile in October 2019 and which are currently dormant.[8]

During the long timeline used in this work, we can see that this disillusioned generation joined the job market after an explosive phase of HE expansion in the previous decade, with an important 'delayed effect' and 'anomic potential' (Coleman, 1965) that Bourdain's sociology describes as a 'hysteresis effect'. In other words, they had late access to a means – HE qualifications – that was no longer in any condition to materialise young people's aspirations and expectations. On the contrary, the job market itself had been devalued, destroying the promise and *illusio* of the cultural goal created by society's transformations and modernisation. The generation that was the first to go on to HE in their families and then also the first to enter the technical-professional job market has become disillusioned with this promise and the means offered to achieve it (HE), entering into a state of Mertonian anomie. Interacting with an additional group of socioeconomic, political and cultural factors, as dealt with in other chapters of this book, the 'anomic potential' of this disillusioned generation was activated and expressed in the protests of October 2019 in Chile.

Before and after the uprising, there have certainly been other solutions implemented and re-implemented to deal with anomie. For example, there has been conformity with both the goal and the means, something accepted by the heirs of economic, social and cultural capital who have continued to believe in their own effort and merits. Alternatively, there have also been responses involving separation, innovation and ritualism that, at an individual and micro-social level, have branched off from these but unquestioningly adapted to society's order. For the most part, the disillusioned generation has rebelled against the system, actively rejecting the cultural goals and educational means that have fed the *illusio* of social mobility and integration over the last thirty years of those who have benefited from Chilean society's capitalist-democratic transformation and modernisation. At the gateway to this generational phenomenon, then, is Bourdieu's phrase:

> These young people, whose social identity and self-image have been undermined by a social system and an education system that have fobbed them off with worthless paper, can find no other way of restoring their personal and social integrity than by a total refusal.
>
> (Bourdieu, 1984: 144)

Notes

1 The research leading to this essay was supported by Project N° 1180746, funded by the Chilean National Fund for Scientific and Technological Development (FONDECYT).
2 Centro de Estudios Públicos (CEP), National Public Opinion Study, July–August 2017.
3 This is reflected in two documents on the commitment of the political-technical and academic elite to education: *Una política para el desarrollo de la educación superior en la década de los noventa* (1990) and *Los desafíos de la educación chilena frente al Siglo XXI* (1994).
4 This calculation is based on a sample of university degrees including acting/theatre studies, architecture, biochemistry, law, economics, computer engineering, medicine, primary school teaching, psychology and sociology. Higher Education Department, Chilean Ministry of Education, *Mi Futuro, Estadísticas* by Carrera, 2021 (in-house).
5 I use this term, adapted from Bourdieu, not only to refer to a mere 'illusion' – something that is not really true, suggested by the imagination or a play of the senses – but also to something that is the complete opposite. It represents a belief that people maintain in the games they play in everyday life that allows them to take their rules and aims seriously. In other words, *illusio* creates the social value of the game itself (Bourdieu, 1993).
6 Interview with Giorgio Jackson, *El País*, Madrid, October 10th 2011.
7 It is likely that this survey, carried out almost a month after the uprising on October 18th and the massive march on October 25th 2019, overrepresents those who are relatively younger, more educated and more politically committed to the protests.

8 This is not the time or place to present our interpretation of the events that occurred after October 18th 2019. However, it is evident that this could also be applied to the majority of the members of the constituent convention, elected on May 16th and 17th 2021. They have also completed or dropped out of HE, a significant number are young adults with degrees or technical qualifications, some of them come from non-selective institutions and, in general, they rebel against a system that, they allege, has deprived them of their place in the order of deserved material and symbolic recognition. Paradoxically, this disillusioned generation now holds part of the constituent power in Chile and is on track to become the new political elite, but one that this time emerges from humble beginnings.

References

Boliver, V. (2011) 'Expansion, Differentiation, and the Persistence of Social Class Inequalities in British Higher Education', *Higher Education* 61(3): 229–242.
Bourdieu, P. (1984) *Distinction: A Social Critique of the Judgement of Taste*. Cambridge, MA: Harvard University Press.
Bourdieu, P. (1990) *The Logic of Practice*. Cambridge: Polity.
Bourdieu, P. (1993) *The Field of Cultural Production*. Cambridge: Polity.
Bourdieu, P. and J.J. Passeron (2009) *Los Herederos: Los Estudiantes y la Cultura*. Buenos Aires: Siglo Veintiuno Editores.
Bravo, J. (2020) *Evolución y características del Subempleo por Competencias de Trabajadores con Educación Superior*. Santiago: CLAPES-UC.
Bravo, J. (2021) *Sobrecalificados: La precaria recuperación del empleo de los graduados de educación superior*. Santiago: CLAPES-UC.
Brunner, J.J. (1998) 'Malestar en la sociedad chilena: ¿de qué, exactamente, estamos hablando?', *Estudios Públicos* 72: 173–198.
Brunner, J.J. (2006a) 'Impresiones culturales del Chile actual', in A. de Toro (ed.) *Cartografías y estrategias de la "postmodernidad" y la "postcolonialidad" en Latinoamérica: "Hibridez" y "Globalización"* ', pp. 185–194. Madrid and Frankfurt: Iberoamericana, Vervuert.
Brunner, J.J. (2006b) 'Chile: Ecología social del cambio Cultural', *Anuario Ininco* 18(1): 1–16.
Brunner, J.J. (2018) 'Sobre las contradicciones culturales del liberalismo y sus malestares', *Estudios Públicos* 150: 161–233.
Burris, B.H. (1983) 'The Human Effects of Underemployment', *Social Problems* 31(1): 96–110.
Canales, M.F. Guajardo and V. Orellana (2020) 'La elite del llano: De la promesa a las desilusiones en la trayectoria postsecundaria de los jóvenes de la nueva clase media', *Ultima década* 28(53): 78–102.
Carrillo, F., S. Espinoza and A. Valenzuela (2018) *Mercado laboral y educación en Chile: Principales tendencias y resultados en 2015*. Santiago: Comisión Nacional de Productividad.
Chiroleu, A. and M. Marquina (2017) 'Democratisation or Credentialism? Public Policies of Expansion of Higher Education in Latin America', *Policy Reviews in Higher Education* 1(2): 139–160.

Cociña, M., R. Frei and O. Larrañaga (2017) *Desiguales: Origen, cambio y desafíos de la brecha social en Chile*. Santiago: UNDP.
Coleman, J.S. (1965) 'Introduction: Education and Political Development', in J.S. Coleman (ed.) *Education and Political Development*, pp. 3–32. Princeton: Princeton University Press.
Collins, R. (2011) 'Credential Inflation and the Future of Universities', *Italian Journal of Sociology of Education* 2: 228–251.
Crozier, M., S.P. Huntington and J. Watanuki (1975) *The Crisis of Democracy*. New York: New York University Press.
Deflem, M. and R.A. Triplett (2018) 'Anomie, Strain, and Opportunity Structure: Robert K. Merton's Paradigm of Deviant Behavior', in R.A. Triplett (ed.) *The Handbook of the History and Philosophy of Criminology*, pp. 140–155. Malden, MA: Wiley-Blackwell.
ECLAC-UNESCO (1992) *Equidad y transformación productiva: Un enfoque integrado*. Santiago: ECLAC-UNESCO.
Geschwender, J.A. (1964) 'Social Structure and the Negro Revolt: An Examination of Some Hypotheses', *Social Forces* 43(2): 248–256.
Jara Villarroel, C. (2020) *¿Aspiraciones cumplidas o abandono del Estado? Percepciones sobre el Estado desde los sectores medios de primera generación*. Santiago: MA Thesis in Sociology of Development, University of Chile.
Merton, R.K. (1969) *Social Theory and Social Structure*. New York: The Free Press.
MORI-FIEL (2020) *Barómetro del Trabajo*. https://cut.cl/cutchile/wp-content/uploads/2020/01/Barometro-parte-II.pdf.
Neundorf, A. and K. Smets (2017) *Political Socialization and the Making of Citizens*. Oxford: Oxford Handbooks Online in Political Science.
NUDESOC (2020) *Núcleo de Sociología Contingente: Informe de resultados oficial Encuesta Zona Cero*. Santiago: NUDESOC.
OECD (2006) *PISA 2006: Science Competencies for Tomorrow's World: Volume 1 Analysis*. Paris: Organisation for Economic Co-operation and Development.
OECD (2019) *Education at a Glance 2019*. Paris: Organisation for Economic Co-Operation and Development.
Ramos Matus, C.F. (2018) *Decisiones educativas y valoración de la educación superior en la trayectoria académica de los profesionales primera generación universitaria*. Santiago: Professional Thesis in Sociology, University of Chile.
Reyes, C. and J. Vallejo (2013) *Los días que avanzaron años: El movimiento estudiantil 2011 desde la perspectiva de sus dirigentes*. Santiago: Ceibo Ediciones.
Ubilla, S.S., A.S. Pérez, L.M. Leibe, B.R. López, J. Arce-Riffo and E.M. Vera (2019) 'Una mirada al movimiento feminista en Chile del año 2018: Hitos, agenda y desafíos', *Iberoamericana. América Latina-España-Portugal* 19(72): 223–245.
Vásquez Palma, O.A. (2017) *Educación superior y movilidad social en universidades privadas de baja selectividad: El caso chileno*. Santiago: PhD Thesis in Social Sciences, University of Chile.

4 Social policies, uncertainty and social unrest in Chile

Rossana Castiglioni

Introduction

In June 2000, the film 'The Perfect Storm' premiered. Based on a true story, it tells of Captain Billy Tyne, who tries to sail his small fishing boat through a terrible storm.[1] In October 1991, as is normal in the northern hemisphere at that time of year, a moderately intense cyclone became significantly stronger given the difference in temperature between a front of cold water and a hot and humid one. This system of low pressure worsened as it moved towards the United States and this mix of meteorological factors – occurring only once every fifty to one hundred years – caused a 'perfect storm'.

Like the events that inspired this film, Chile also faced a perfect sociopolitical storm in the month of October but this time in 2019. In September of that year, President Sebastián Piñera's government announced an increase of four US cents in the price of underground tickets. This price rise was accompanied by some very unfortunate declarations from important members of the government. For example, Finance Minister Juan A. Fontaine recommended that underground users got up earlier if they wanted to pay less, while the Minister of Finance, Felipe Larraín, said that deflation was good news for romantics because flowers had gone down in price. Both these declarations and the price hike were widely criticised and, in the following weeks, different student groups organised protests at underground stations, calling on users to dodge fares (Castiglioni, 2019).

In just a few days, what began as isolated protests turned into widespread demonstrations lasting several weeks, leading to what came to be known as the social uprising. Demonstrations came to a head on 25 October 2019, when the biggest march to ever take place in Chile occurred. That day, 1.2 million Chileans came together all over the country to manifest their discontent. In total, just a month after the social uprising, 4.3 million protesters had taken part in demonstrations (*La Tercera*, 18 November 2019). To put this number into perspective, it is worth remembering that, during

DOI: 10.4324/9781003254355-5

the 2017 presidential elections, only around 3.8 million Chileans voted for Sebastián Piñera.

These protests took the government by surprise. After the social uprising in October, different high-ranking politicians had, visibly distressed, admitted that they had no idea such demonstrations would take place or about how much discontent there actually was. President Piñera indicated that 'we definitely went through something no one expected, that had never happened before. . . . People's discontent grew and grew and was suddenly and explosively expressed' (*La Nación*, 12 December 2019). For her part, government spokesperson Karla Rubilar, an experienced politician, admitted that 'we didn't see this level of discontent and frustration coming. I think we have to start by recognising that all of us have been completely overwhelmed by what has happened' (*24horas*, 3 November 2019). Similarly, the former Minister of Finance said that "we couldn't comprehend what was going on" (*El Mercurio*, 28 October 2019).

The hostility reflected in the protests was in strong contrast to the way the government and other politicians viewed the state of the country at the time. This was seen ten days before the social uprising in President Piñera's declaration that, 'in the midst of a Latin America in turmoil, we find Chile, a country that is a true oasis, with a stable democracy and growth. We're creating 176,000 jobs a year and wages are improving' (*La Tercera*, 8 October 2019). Analysts, scholars and politicians from different parties also singled out Chile as a country with a full-blown democracy, stable institutions and rules of the game, an outstanding economic performance and as having made important improvements in different social indicators, particularly regarding reducing poverty.

Why then did this oasis become a desert? What explains this social uprising? What factors played a role in its occurrence? Like any complex socio-political crisis, it is impossible to reduce its beginnings to a single explanation. In fact, it was undoubtedly the convergence of different factors that led to the social uprising, making it a phenomenon that can only be explained in terms of different configurations. As opposed to other kinds of crisis, however, in which citizens react spontaneously to price hikes or unpopular measures, the causes of the Chilean social uprising were not short-term ones. In fact, in my opinion, this phenomenon has structural roots, with causes that had been brewing for decades. That is why it is not at all surprising that one of the protestors' favourite slogan was 'It's not 30 pesos but 30 years'.

In this chapter I argue that one of the keys to understanding the social uprising lies in the high levels of uncertainty faced by middle-income sectors. Reducing poverty brought with it an increase in the number of people and homes with an income that, although placing them above the poverty line, still made them vulnerable. According to official figures in 2018, at the dawn of the social uprising, half of all workers earned less than US$ 540 a month (INE, 2018b). The average monthly income per capita for workers was US$ 770, while the average pension for Chilean men was US$ 432 and for women US$ 260. Only 1.7 per cent of all Chileans earned more than US$ 4,000.[2]

Sectors with a variable average income spend more than they earn and are heavily in debt. They have no capacity to assume unexpected costs and so face increasing uncertainty every single day. They have low-quality jobs and depend on their own – or their families' – ability to pay for any unexpected expenses. In addition, they usually find it incredibly difficult to pay for medical attention, which is already excessively expensive and that normally exceeds their budgets. Even though their income is obviously insufficient, they are not eligible for social security, since these benefits are usually means-tested.

In a context in which politicians and institutions of representation have few members and even less legitimacy, both the democratic deficit and the number of 'critical citizens' who resort to protests to express their discontent have increased (Castiglioni and Rovira Kaltwasser, 2016). The political class has not been able or has not wanted to satisfy the heterogeneous complaints of the middle-income sectors or reduce their levels of insecurity and uncertainty. This meant that both tension and discontent have accumulated over time and ended up being expressed through the 2019 social uprising.

This chapter is organised as follows. The next section analyses the social and political context in which the social uprising occurred in Chile. The second section examines and typifies the expansion of the insecure and discontent middle-income sectors. The third section identifies three areas in which this vulnerability is visible: work, debt and the inability to deal with unexpected expenses. Therefore, this class becomes more and more unsatisfied with democracy, widening the so-called democratic deficit. Finally, the last section discusses the current scenario going forward.

The social and political context prior to the uprising

'Our country is a true oasis'. This is how President Sebastián Piñera described his country just ten days before the social uprising. As exaggerated as his declaration may seem, it was not actually the result of a moment of presidential insanity. In fact, the vision of Chile as a successful and thriving country was widely shared by experts, politicians and analysts, both Chilean and foreign and, in truth, the majority of the empirical evidence seemed to support this idea.

Over the last few decades, Chile has figured in every ranking as one of the most solid and consolidated democracies in Latin America (Coppedge et al., 2020).

Moreover, at the time of the uprising, these all described Chile as a democracy as established as exemplary ones in the northern hemisphere. Its political institutions and rules of the game showed a high level of stability and were respected by the majority of both politicians and citizens. Political parties, for their part, had been highly institutionalised since the transition to democracy. As Nolte said in 2003, 'The Chilean political system has worked much better than expected and Chilean presidential rule has been more stable than other similar systems on the continent' (Nolte, 2003: 44).

At the same time, the Chilean economy had shown consistently above-average growth in the region, as well as macroeconomic indicators accounting for this solid performance. The gross domestic product per capita also experienced a marked increase: in 1990, it was US$ 10,203 but, due to constant growth, it reached US$ 22,104 in 2018, bringing it much more in line with European countries such as Greece (US$ 23,450) and Portugal (US$ 27,035) than the Latin American average of US$ 12,745 per capita (Castiglioni and Rovira Kaltwasser, 2016; Coppedge et al., 2020).

Finally, different social indicators have obviously improved since the transition to democracy in 1990. Poverty and destitution have gone down considerably and healthcare coverage has increased. On the other hand, primary and secondary education has become practically universal and university enrolment has experienced an extraordinary increase. Finally, life expectancy at birth is now similar to that of developed countries and infant mortality has continued to fall.

This combination of factors – in other words, a solid democracy, a thriving economy and an improvement in social indicators – transformed Chile into a kind of model for the rest of Latin America to emulate, as well as creating demand for several of the country's specialists and politicians as consultants for neighbouring countries, advising those undertaking different kinds of reforms. Nevertheless, in the years prior to the social uprising, several different alarm bells had sounded, which the Chilean political class either was unable to interpret or simply chose to ignore. Gradually, these emerged in three main areas (Castiglioni and Rovira Kaltwasser, 2016). Firstly, identification with political parties and coalitions has been declining since the transition to democracy. According to a survey by the Centro de Estudios Públicos (CEP), in 1993, 70 per cent of Chilean adults identified with a political party but by 2019, this had gone down to a startlingly low 19 per cent.[3] These opinion polls also showed an even greater and more consistent decline both in their trust of politicians and of political institutions, such as the government, parliament and political parties.

Secondly, Chile has suffered a notable drop in electoral participation. In 1989, in the first presidential election to be held since the collapse of democracy in 1973, approximately 85 per cent of the electorate voted. In contrast, since 2012, electoral participation has been around or under 50 per cent.[4] This drop is truly dramatic, even on a global scale. In a study from October 2017, the United Nations Development Programme (UNDP) indicated that, in the last twenty-five years, Chile had experienced the second largest drop in electoral participation globally (36 per cent), a number only beaten by that of Madagascar (UNDP, 2017a). Although it is true that different modern democracies, from the United States to Switzerland, have high levels of electoral abstention, the Chilean case is dramatic because of its resounding drop. The enactment of the 'Automatic Registration and Voluntary Voting Law' in January 2012 did not help reverse the continuous decline in voter turnout that began in the early 1990s.

Thirdly, since 2006 and the so-called 'Penguin Revolution' involving demonstrations by middle-school students, the number of demonstrations has increased and formal and institutionalised ways of channelling discontent and (re)politicising inequalities have decreased (Castiglioni and Rovira Kaltwasser, 2016). Successive waves of protests have tackled the heterogeneous demands associated with different areas of social politics and socio-structural categories, from pensions, work, healthcare and education to territorial, gender and ethnic inequalities, to mention just a few.

There is no doubt that the formal and informal rules of the game account for an important number of the political representation problems that besiege Chile today. In addition, it is obvious that both institutions and politicians have had great trouble responding to the growing discontent in society (Joignant, 2012). For many, the sacred institutional architecture of the 1980 Constitution, drawn up under the Pinochet authoritarian regime, includes different institutional obstacles and barriers aimed at maintaining the status quo and making it difficult to introduce structural changes (Castiglioni, 2005; Coddou and Couso, 2009; Heiss, 2020; Fuentes, 2015; Siavelis, 2016).

Therefore, Chilean institutional resilience and the absence of formal ways for channelling discontent have ended up spilling out onto the streets and into the government, with their roots in a Constitution that was not drawn up as part of a deliberative democratic process.

Perhaps as a result, the social uprising appeared to bring to the table not only the demands for socioeconomic changes but also the call for a new democratic Constitution. These demands indicate that the Constitution should be the result of a deliberative process that is legitimate and does not reflect the sins of the past. The aim is for this new Constitution to eliminate the institutional arrangements designed to obstruct change, therefore harmonising with a Chilean society that has already changed itself.

In summary, although Chile has made important advances since the transition to democracy, the legitimacy of its politicians and political institutions shows clear signs of deterioration and political participation has experienced an exceptionally high drop. In this scenario, faced with a lack of institutional measures to make their increasing discontent visible and therefore to pressure the government into change, citizens have started to favour protests. However, these changes have taken too long to arrive and in general, when they have, have been parametric, incremental or gradual.

The expansion of the middle-income sectors

One of Chile's main achievements as far as social indicators go is connected to an obvious reduction in poverty. Effectively, poverty based on income used to include 68 per cent of the country's total population, but by 2017 this number had dropped to 8.6 per cent (MDSF-UNDP, 2020). This impressive leap forward was the result of different factors, including a combination of social policies focused on the most vulnerable people and homes and a solid economic performance to finance this. At the same time, this decrease in poverty brought with it an increasing number of people whose income placed them above the poverty line. This change created a debate that has not yet been resolved about what being part of this 'new middle class' actually means (Barozet and Espinoza, 2016).

The concept of the 'middle class' is often hard to pin down, partly because self-perception tends to distance it from the more objective indicators of income and socioeconomic level. As Barozet indicates

> the concept of the middle class today reflects many different realities and it is important to take note of this variety because, when reflecting on what we are and what we want to be – above all in these times of economic and political uncertainty – it is common to blend categories.
> (Barozet, 2017)

This is why I refer to *middle-income sectors* and not *the middle class* in this chapter, in order to be more specific and narrow down the focus.

Different reports and studies aim to determine the income threshold necessary for a person or home to be considered as having an average income. In this chapter, I will consider the definition provided by the study 'Towards a Definition of the Middle Class in Chile', according to which average income corresponds to homes whose total income is 1.5 to six times above the poverty line each year. In a home with four people, the 2017 equivalent is a total monthly income of between 626,021 and 2,504,083 Chilean pesos, in other words between US$ 964 and US$ 3,856 per month per household or between US$ 241 and US$ 964 per month per capita (LyD, 2019). This classification is particularly relevant due to the fact that it was based on the same 'Protected Middle Class' programme that President Piñera's government had implemented in May 2019 (*La Tercera*, 19 June 2020). It is worth noting that this definition includes the World Bank's conceptualisation of the same, as well as recommendations from the Chilean government's Commission for Measuring Poverty.

According to the previously mentioned study and the definition suggested, the majority of the Chilean population earns an average income (LyD, 2019: 3). This study also indicates that the country's growth has been important: in 2006, 43.2 per cent of the population was in this segment, in 2013 this number had grown to 56.6 per cent and by 2017 it was 65.4 per cent. At the same time, the study indicates that the lower middle class includes those who have a family income 1.5 (US$ 964) to three times (US$ 1,928) above the poverty line for a household of four people – in other words, between US$ 241 and US$ 482 per capita.

Within the universe of average income sectors, there are more people with average to low incomes, who represent 63.1 per cent of the average income level and 42.5 per cent of the country's total population. Many of these average to low-income sectors are households run by women (44 per cent) and old age pensioners (40.7 per cent), with an average of 9.6 years of schooling and, as we will see later on, generally insecure and/or informal jobs (LyD, 2019: 3–4).

As Barozet and Espinoza indicate

> if purchasing power was the key for characterizing middle classes, Chilean middle-income sectors would hardly correspond to a family with its own house and access to quality health and education services. Yet, following international standards that define middle strata as the group that falls within +/-25 percent of median income, the lower bracket falls under the poverty line.
>
> (Barozet and Espinoza, 2016: 98)

Therefore, a large number of middle-income sectors are unstable, with high levels of vulnerability and uncertainty. This vulnerability, however, does not translate into substantial state support.

For poverty-struck and destitute households, 17.9 per cent and 23.5 per cent of their total income, respectively, comes from benefits. However, among all the homes under the poverty line, only 3 per cent of total income comes from benefits (MDSF, 2019: 20). What is most striking is that, in the case of middle- to low-income families, only 4 per cent of total monetary income comes from benefits (LyD, 2019: 5). These numbers reflect the fact that subsidies and benefits in Chile are mainly means-tested. In this sense, there is evidence that, in Chile and other Latin American countries, middle-income sectors pay more than they receive in social services (UNDP, 2019: 247),

Job insecurity in the middle-income sector and the democratic deficit

The increase in job insecurity in these sectors is reflected not only in their lack of income, but also in at least three additional areas, namely their job situation, debt and their (in)ability to finance unexpected costs. Job flexibility in the Chilean market, associated with the market reforms the country has adopted in previous decades, has had an important effect on job quality and on the vulnerability of Chilean workers (Stecher and Sisto, 2019: 38). Indeed, the average Chilean wage is relatively low for the country's level of development and family income is variable. In addition, contractual conditions are unstable (especially for women, old age pensioners and people with less education) which results in job insecurity. After the transition, this situation was exacerbated by employment legislation that is considered some of the most hostile in the world to trade unions. This legislation restricts collective bargaining at a sectorial level and includes an important number of obstacles to the right to strike (Azócar Simonet and Cruz González, 2015; Sehnbruch, 2012).

Although it is true that Chile possesses one of the most formal employment markets in Latin America, there are still more than 2.4 million informal workers and 1.3 million freelancers (INE, 2018a). Chile also has the highest number of short-term contracted workers in the OECD (27 per cent) after Colombia, putting it well above the OECD average of 11.8 per cent.[5] Of the total number of part-time workers, 44 per cent work part-time but not by choice, compared to the OECD's 14 per cent.[6]

The numbers also show that employment has become more insecure over time. In 1999, 83 per cent of Chilean workers had indefinite work contracts; ten years later, this number had gone down to 66 per cent (Dirección del Trabajo, 2019). This situation is even more complex for the heads of middle- to low-income households, who have comparatively low levels of employment (64 per cent) and high levels of insecure and/or informal work, with only 40 per cent having a job contract (LyD, 2019: 3–4).

Another important source of uncertainty is linked to the Chilean population's high levels of debt. Considering the difference between households' average per capita monthly spending and income (excluding mortgages or rent), all the quintiles, with the exception of the higher income one (made up of individuals who earn more than US$ 1,432 per month), spend more than they earn (INE, 2018b). Almost half of all spending is on food, transport, household expenses and bills, while 14 per cent goes on healthcare and education (INE, 2018b).

On the other hand, Chilean households' level of debt has gone up over the last few decades, which has resulted in almost 35 per cent of adult Chileans defaulting on their debts (Miranda *et al.*, 2020). According to official figures, in 2017, 66 per cent of Chilean households were in debt and 55 per cent of this was due to consumer credit. As opposed to other countries, access to credit in Chile is available to households with relatively low incomes and to individuals with little financial education (Miranda *et al.*, 2020). Of the total number of homes at financial risk – in other words, who use more than 30 per cent of their income to pay interest on or to pay off debt – almost half come from the five lowest income quintiles. This is in contrast to the 22 per cent of the deciles with the highest incomes (Pinto Gutiérrez, 2016).

Job insecurity in middle-income sectors is usually most evident when these families and people have to deal with unexpected expenses or situations. This problem is particularly serious when it comes to healthcare. There is no doubt that the levels of healthcare in Chile are high and have improved over time. The health system reform approved by the government of President Ricardo Lagos (2000–2016), which introduced the Universal Access to Healthcare Plan and Explicit Healthcare Guarantees (AUGE-GES), guaranteed speedy access to medical attention with accredited providers. This made it easier for any patient meeting the criteria to access healthcare for a set of pre-established illnesses that has been significantly expanded over time (Castiglioni, 2018).

This reform was a huge step forward for those affected by 1 of the 85 diseases that currently qualify for and are covered under the plan. However, one of the main aims of this reform – to promote a more equitable and supportive system – remains unfulfilled. This is due to the fact that the main measure in this sense, involving the creation of a compensation fund, did not get enough support in Congress and was not approved. The aim of this fund was to reduce inequality and promote solidarity by distributing the costs of the AUGE-GES plan between members of the public and private healthcare sub-systems (Castiglioni, 2018). Therefore, despite the changes, the Chilean healthcare system has continued to be highly segmented and with significant differences in the quality of care between sub-systems and beneficiaries, depending on level of income and ability to pay. This is also made worse by the fact that the system involves workers paying 7 per cent of their taxable income to private or for-profit public institutions, with those in the private system also allowed to pay additional amounts. This creates a paradox, with the individuals with the highest incomes who use the private sub-system being those with fewer health problems but who pay the most (Castiglioni, 2005). In addition, some studies also show important differences between the treatment public and private sub-system beneficiaries receive, as well as obvious differences in access to specialists, dental work and tests (UNDP, 2017b: 337).

Another big problem with the healthcare system is its elevated cost, even for the 78 per cent of Chileans in the public healthcare sub-system (FONASA). The only FONASA beneficiaries exempt from paying are those without any income at all or whose income is no higher than US$ 337 a month and/or who receive a basic state pension. The rest of those in the public healthcare system must make co-payments depending on their income level, including those who make the minimum wage (Castiglioni, 2019). It is worth emphasising that Chile is the country with the third highest out-of-pocket expenses in the OECD, which is why households finance an average of 35.1 per cent of their total healthcare expenses (*24horas*, 5 July 2019). Therefore, when it comes to a life-threatening illness or having to spend money on medication not covered by the healthcare plans, it is usually impossible for them to meet these costs from their family budget. That is why it is common for people to go further into debt or hold charity events or raffles to raise money for these out-of-pocket expenses, or even sell their few belongings.

On the other hand, the expansion of the middle class with job insecurity has occurred in a context in which the problems of democratic legitimacy analysed in the second part of this chapter have gotten worse and the 'democratic deficit' has widened. Norris indicates that democracies

> are more likely to endure and flourish where there is an equilibrium between citizens' aspirations for democracy (measured by how much people value democratic ideals and reject autocratic alternatives) and its perceived supply (monitored by public satisfaction with the democratic performance of their own country). The gap between aspiration and satisfaction is captured by the concept of democratic deficits.
>
> (Norris, 2011: 4–5)

In this sense, Chile has experienced a drop both in the level of support for democracy as a political regime and in satisfaction with how it works. In 1999, 62 per cent of Chileans said they supported democracy, but in 2017, just before the uprising, this figure had dropped to 52 per cent. As far as levels of satisfaction with democracy are concerned, there was also a drop from the 26 per cent in 1999 who said they were satisfied to 11 per cent in 2017.[7] As a result, the democratic deficit has increased.

It is in this context that the so-called 'critical citizens' emerge – in other words, dissatisfied democrats who have become more and more discontent with the performance of government institutions of representation (Castiglioni and Rovira Kaltwasser, 2016; Norris, 1999). This dissatisfaction is reflected in dramatically lower levels of identification with political parties and trust in institutions. In 1993, 70 per cent of Chileans identified with a political party or coalition, while in 2017 this number had dropped to 29 per cent. Trust in institutions during democracy has been particularly low. In effect, in 2017, only 11 per cent of Chileans trusted the government and only 6 per cent trusted Congress and the different political parties. These numbers continued to drop after the uprising to 5.3 per cent and 2 per cent, respectively.[8]

This frustration and dissatisfaction have become apparent over the last fifteen years in demonstrations. After a long period of social fragmentation and demobilisation, Chile started to experience a wave of protests as a result of different complaints, from 2006 when middle-school students started to protest to 2011, when university students protested in favour of public, free and quality education. Many of the protestors' demands were general or symbolic, fitting under an umbrella as wide as to include dignity, equality and social justice. However, a large number of the complaints also referred to specifically recognising the call for better wages, the end of privately administered pension funds and better access to medication, among others. This was reflected in the surveys taken to gauge public opinion. In fact, in a survey carried out between October and November 2018 that excluded topics related to public safety and corruption, every measure chosen as a priority by more than 20 per cent of those polled was connected to social demands: pensions (48 per cent), healthcare (37 per cent), education (34 per cent), employment (23 per cent) and poverty (20 per cent).[9]

In summary, the social uprising of 2019 brought to the fore not only these demands for heterogeneous but somewhat vague changes, but also a dissatisfaction that had been accumulating for decades. In the context of the October 2019 protests, a diverse group of complaints from both social groups and individuals emerged in the public arena, which were not taken up by or capitalised on by traditional political parties. These demands were partly motivated by the existence of vulnerable middle-class sectors, whose income is insufficient, who are in debt, who have low-quality jobs and who find it extremely difficult to finance emergencies and/or unexpected expenses. This becomes particularly evident when they have to deal with unexpected expenses related to healthcare or life-threatening illnesses.

Conclusion

The 2019 social uprising has made it clear that Chile has not been able to resolve the political legitimacy crisis that has been brewing for decades. Electoral participation has fallen since the transition, membership of political parties is waning and trust in democratic institutions is scandalously low. After weeks of repression, unfortunate declarations by the president and limited compensatory measures that did nothing more than worsen the protests and discontent, the leaders of the main parties agreed to negotiate a political way out of the crisis, which included drawing up a new Constitution. In this context, as a result of a tense day of negotiations in Congress, the Social Peace Agreement was agreed on in the early morning of November 15 2019.

As a result of this agreement, on October 25 2020, a plebiscite was held, with overwhelming results. Turnout was 51 per cent; 78 per cent of voters who went to the polls supported the idea of a new constitutional text and 79 per cent voted for this to be written by a constitutional committee comprised 155 elected members.[10] It is worth highlighting that this involves a Constitution written using a 'blank slate' and which is not based on any previous version of the same. For any measure to be included in the new Constitution, it has to have the support of two-thirds of the constitutional convention. This convention has equal numbers of men and women and 17 places reserved for representatives of native people. The constitutional text drawn up by this committee must be ratified by an exit referendum that will probably be held in the second half of 2022.

The election of convention members, for its part, took place on 15 and 16 May 2021, together with the election of national deputies (governors, mayors and councillors). The results of this election reveal a complex scenario, with a low turnout (barely 43 per cent of the eligible population) and votes dispersed widely. These elections involved an unprecedented number of independent candidates and the consolidation of left-wing groups based around the Frente Amplio alliance. This alliance is setting itself up as an ever more powerful political force, to the detriment of the former Concertación coalition, and has managed to defeat well-established candidates belonging to the two large centre-right and centre-left coalitions.

As a result of this election, the new Constitution will be written over the next few months by a heterogeneous constitutional convention, 42 per cent of which is made up of independent constituents, many of them without political affiliation or previous political experience. This scenario is paradoxical. Deep-rooted political transformations in democratic contexts need strong, institutionalised political parties that attract members and add legitimacy to complex processes. Nevertheless, in Chile, a mixture of independents and party representatives who enjoy low levels of public confidence will head up a process conceived as the main way to deal with the perfect socio-political storm. This is why the outcome of this constitutional process in Chile is still highly uncertain.

The current context poses two additional challenges. On one hand, for an important number of citizens, including the middle-income sector with insecure jobs, the new Constitution could involve changes aimed at resolving their everyday problems of access to social services and insufficient income. A study by the Market Research and Public Opinion Association[11] shows that the three most important rights that Chileans think should be guaranteed in the new Constitution are the right to education (61 per cent), healthcare coverage (54 per cent) and social security (48 per cent). The study also shows that 63 per cent of Chileans trust that the constituent process will resolve the problems associated with pensions, the quality of healthcare, education, employment and wages. For 61 per cent, the hope is that the process also brings positive changes both to democracy and to how social and economic life is regulated.

The fact that the population has pinned their hopes and expectations on the new Constitution is a double-edged sword, since these can be easily shot down. This situation can be compared to what Daniel Lerner *et al.* call a revolution of increasing frustrations and/or expectations. In an analysis of the Turkish modernisation process, Lerner and Robinson indicate that this country experienced a revolution of rising expectations when people's aspirations for a better life could not be met, unleashing an accumulation of frustrations that turned into progressive political instability (Lerner and Robinson, 1960).

In the case of Chile, an important discourse was promoted by a large part of the traditional political elite, positioning Chile as a country with a solid democracy and booming economy that had achieved excellent results in different social indicators. This contrasts heavily with the feeling of defencelessness, job insecurity and vulnerability experienced by 43 per cent of the country's total population in the so-called lower middle class. The hopes of these sectors are pinned on a constituent process that will find it difficult to resolve the population's everyday problems. The biggest challenge is how to contain and manage the growing expectations that may not actually be met in the end, creating new conflicts.

The other challenge Chile has to deal with is the Covid-19 pandemic and its socioeconomic fallout. A political class in the midst of a profound legitimacy crisis has also had to deal with the worst health crisis in modern history. Since the emergence of Covid-19, the number of demonstrations has decreased, probably because of fear of the virus more than a lack of conviction. While the population waits hopefully for the constituent process to resolve the majority of the problems that affect them, surveys also show that only 16 per cent believe that their financial situation is good or very good, while 35 per cent say that that it is bad or very bad and only 25 per cent think their financial situation will improve.[12]

Job insecurity among middle-income sectors has become even more obvious during the pandemic. Covid-19 seems to have worked as a kind of echo chamber for existing problems. Today more than ever, the pandemic has revealed the fragility of those with low-quality jobs, who lack savings and who have problems accessing services. In this respect, the World Bank has warned that lower middle-income families are so vulnerable that Covid-19 could put 2 million Chileans under the poverty line in the space of just a few months, due to a possible increase in unemployment and the high costs associated with life-threatening illnesses (Inchauste et al., 2020).

In summary, despite politicians' willingness to look for a way out of the Chilean legitimacy crisis and to recognise that there must be changes to the inequality in access and opportunities, there is still a long road to travel. In an adverse macroeconomic context with weakened political parties, a broad and transversal agreement is needed, which will require a huge amount of generosity on both sides. Only through this can we hope for a favourable outcome to this crisis.

Notes

1 I would like to thank David Altman, Camila Arza, José Joaquín Brunner, Juliana Martínez-Franzoni, Claudio Fuentes, Sara Niedzwiecki and Carmen Midaglia, Carlos Peña, Patricio Silva and my colleagues from PolSoc (the Latin American Network for Social Policy Analysis) for their comments and suggestions.
2 All the income-related data come from the National Institution of Statistics' Supplementary Survey on Income, available at www.ine.cl/estadisticas/ingresos-y-gastos/esi. The dollar exchange rate was taken from the Chilean Central Bank's website and is equivalent to the annual average.
3 www.cepchile.cl/cep/site/edic/base/port/encuestasCEP.html
4 https://historico.servel.cl/
5 https://data.oecd.org/emp/temporary-employment.htm#indicator-chart
6 https://stats.oecd.org/Index.aspx?DataSetCode=INVPT_I
7 www.cepchile.cl/encuestaCEP
8 www.cepchile.cl/encuestaCEP
9 www.cepchile.cl/encuestaCEP
10 https://historico.servel.cl/
11 www.aimchile.cl/wp-content/uploads/2021/04/VF-Estudio-Voces-Ciudadanas-para-la-Constituyente.pdf
12 www.cepchile.cl/cep/encuestas-cep/encuestas-2010-2019/1-encuesta-especial-cep-abril-2021

References

Azócar Simonet, R. and A. Cruz González (2015) 'Limitaciones al derecho de huelga en Chile: Los servicios esenciales, el reemplazo de trabajadores y los servicios mínimos en el contexto de la Reforma Laboral', *Revista Chilena de Derecho del Trabajo y de la Seguridad Social* 6(12): 140–161.

Barozet, E. (2017) *¿Es usted de clase media? Probablemente no*. Santiago: CIPER, 10 April.

Barozet, E. and V. Espinoza (2016) 'Current Issues on the Political Representation of Middle Classes in Chile', *Journal of Politics in Latin America* 8(3): 95–123.

Castiglioni, R. (2005) *The Politics of Social Policy Change in Chile and Uruguay: Retrenchment Versus Maintenance, 1973–1998*. London: Routledge.
Castiglioni, R. (2018) 'Explaining Uneven Social Policy Expansion in Democratic Chile', *Latin American Politics and Society* 60(3): 54–76.
Castiglioni, R. (2019) '¿El ocaso del "modelo chileno"?', *Nueva Sociedad* 284: 4–14.
Castiglioni, R. and C. Rovira Kaltwasser (2016) 'Challenges to Political Representation in Contemporary Chile', *Journal of Politics in Latin America* 8(3): 3–24.
Coddou, A. and J. Couso (2009) *Las asignaturas pendientes de la reforma constitucional chilena*. Santiago: ICSO-UDP.
Coppedge, M. et al. (2020) *Data set Varieties of Democracy*. Gothenburg: Department of Political Science, University of Gothenburg.
Dirección del Trabajo (2019) *ENCLA: Informe de Resultados, Novena Encuesta Laboral 2019*. Santiago: Dirección del Trabajo.
Fuentes, C. (2015) 'Shifting the Status Quo: Constitutional Reforms in Chile', *Latin American Politics and Society* 57: 99–122.
Heiss, C. (2020) *¿Por qué necesitamos una nueva Constitución?* Santiago: Aguilar.
Inchauste, G., J. de Hoop and T. Saavedra (2020) *COVID-19: Crisis Could Reverse Years of Growth in Chile's Middle-Class*. Washington, DC: The World Bank.
INE (2018a) *Informalidad Laboral*. Santiago: Instituto Nacional de Estadísticas.
INE (2018b) *Síntesis de Resultados: VIII EPF*. Santiago: Instituto Nacional de Estadísticas.
Joignant, A. (2012) 'El reclamo de las elites: Desencanto, desafección y malestar en Chile', *Revista UDP* 9: 103–105.
Lerner, D. and R. Robinson (1960) 'Swords and Ploughshares: The Turkish Army as a Modernizing Force', *World Politics* 13(1): 19–44.
LyD (2019) *Hacia una Nueva Definición de Clase Media en Chile*. Santiago: Instituto Libertad y Desarrollo.
MDSF (2019) *Informe Desarrollo Social 2019*. Santiago: Ministerio de Desarrollo Social y Familia.
MDSF – UNDP (2020) *Evolución de la pobreza 1990–2017: ¿Cómo ha cambiado Chile?*. Santiago: Ministerio de Desarrollo Social y Familia, United Nations Development Programme.
Miranda, A., R. Montero and H. Talbot-Wright (2020) *Comparación Social y Decisiones de Endeudamiento: Evidencia para Chile*. Santiago: Ministerio de Hacienda.
Nolte, D. (2003) 'El Congreso chileno y su aporte a la consolidación democrática en perspectiva comparada', *Revista de Ciencia Política* 23(2): 43–67.
Norris, P. (1999) 'Introduction: The Growth of Critical Citizens?', in P. Norris (ed.) *Critical Citizens: Global Support for Democratic Government*, pp. 1–30. Oxford: Oxford University Press.
Norris, P. (2011) *Democratic Deficit: Critical Citizens Revisited*. New York: Cambridge University Press.
Pinto Gutiérrez, C. (2016) *El Perfil de los Hogares Más Endeudados en Chile*. Santiago: Universidad del Desarrollo.
Sehnbruch, K. (2012) *Unable to Shape the Political Arena: The Impact of Poor Quality Employment on Unions in Post-Transition Chile*. Santiago: Centre for New Development Thinking.

Siavelis, P. (2016) 'Crisis of Representation in Chile? The Institutional Connection', *Journal of Politics in Latin America* 8(3): 61–93.
Stecher, A. and V. Sisto (2019) 'Trabajo y precarización laboral en el Chile Neoliberal', in K. Araujo (ed.) *Hilos tensados*, pp. 37–82. Santiago: Editorial USACH.
UNDP (2017a) *Diagnóstico sobre la Participación Electoral en Chile*. Santiago: UNDP.
UNDP (2017b) *Desiguales: Orígenes, cambios y desafíos de la brecha social en Chile*. Santiago: UNDP.
UNDP (2019) *Human Development Report 2019: Beyond Income, Beyond Averages, Beyond Today*. New York: UNDP.

5 The socio-political dynamic of the constituent process

Claudio A. Fuentes

Introduction

Since its return to democracy, the case of Chile has been considered exceptional for several different reasons.[1] To start with, this was a pacted transition in which, after it began in 1990, the military continued to play a key role for more than a decade. In addition, it is a case that has held on to a Constitution inherited from the dictatorship for forty years, with only a few adjustments. Together with this, Chile is unprecedented in terms of its economic modernisation and poverty reduction. Finally, it is a case of surprising political party stability. This means that it has even been considered as an example worthy of emulating in terms of its capacity to create governability and establish agreements (Levitsky and Ziblatt, 2018). Since 2019, however, several of these premises have crumbled and the country's political system seems to be less robust than normal. Namely, the injustices of its economic model have led to a cycle of intense protests. What seemed to be a strong and pacted institutionality has ended up in a constituent process that will review the basis of the Republic itself and replace the existing Constitution.

What factors explain this dynamic? Why did the country go from a gradualist strategy of institutional reforms to a more radical strategy of replacing the Constitution? It is true that, after Pinochet's dictatorship established the Constitution in 1980, the main centre-left political forces opted for a strategy of gradual institutional change. Since they never managed to get a significant majority in Congress to replace the Constitution, they chose to carry out partial reforms that eliminated the authoritarian aspects of said normative framework.

During her second government, socialist President Michelle Bachelet (2014–2018) suggested a participative process to draw up a new Constitution. A few days before leaving power, she sent a bill to totally reform the Constitution to Congress. However, the new right-wing government headed up by President Sebastián Piñera (2018–2022) quickly ruled out any debate on a new Constitution. Five days before the government came to power, Home Secretary Andrés Chadwick, in a meeting with some of the country's most important businessmen, clarified his government's road map. With deliberate firmness, he indicated that 'We don't want to move forward with the new Constitution. . . . A Constitution isn't a game, a Constitution isn't just a simple project' (March 15th 2018). A year and a half later, this same government coalition embarked on an unprecedented process of constitutional change. For the first time since 1810, the people had the opportunity to decide whether they wanted to change the Constitution or not (in a referendum held in October 2020). In addition, Chileans had the chance to vote for the members of the constituent convention (in May 2021). Finally, citizens will also vote to ratify the text of the newly written Constitution (in August 2022).

What then explains this unprecedented and even surprising agreement to replace the Constitution? The first, most intuitive answer to this question is pressure from society. The social uprising that occurred on and after October 18th 2019 threatened the interests of the political and economic elite and generated such a level of uncertainty that it led to an agreement to change the Constitution. From October 18th to November 15th of this same year, the situation was highly volatile, with strikes and protests common. This compelled the country's political leaders to find solutions, one of which was to establish an agreement to change the Constitution.

The following question, however, immediately emerges: Why change the Constitution if citizen demands at that time were connected to improving people's quality of life? Why suggest a political and institutional solution to material and social demands? In this chapter, I will try and answer these questions. I will argue that the Chilean constituent process is the result of what I will call the progressive 'constitutionalisation' of society. It is a medium-term process in which certain structural, social and political circumstances changed the status quo in Chile, eventually creating the conditions for constitutional change.

By 'constitutionalisation', I am referring to the process through which politicians and society have come to accept that the majority of Chile's social problems are connected with the way in which society coexists, something reflected in the Constitution. Both social and political dynamics gradually found themselves up against the barriers or blockades set out as part of the constitutional framework. That is why, when the social uprising occurred on October 18th 2019, the situation was ripe for advances to be made on institutional solutions to the social conflict. Changing the Constitution became a way of channelling or driving protests and tackling a series of issues linked to the demand for social rights that had been postponed in the past.

The argument I will develop in this chapter moves away from a single-cause vision that only focuses its attention on one main factor in order to understand the political dynamic. Firstly, I will argue that certain social structural conditions must be taken into consideration, since these have encouraged social demands. Secondly, attention must be paid to certain factors endogenous to the political system (political reforms, intellectual activism and social dialogue initiatives) that both led to the proposals for constitutional change and made them viable. Thirdly, the timeframe of the events establishing the conditions for a change to the status quo must be borne in mind (Pierson, 2004). In the following sections, I will develop my arguments in detail and then draw some tentative conclusions about the Chilean political process and its prospects.

Macro-social transformations and the dynamics of social protest

Protests have been singled out as the main reason why Chile is embarking on a constituent process. Along these lines, the bigger the protests that threaten the elite's interests, the greater the probability that these elites become more amenable to responding with institutional changes. However, as indicated in the introduction, this argument, which seems intuitive, needs more explanation, since the majority of social-citizen demands are based specifically on improving quality of life. A national survey carried out by the Centro de Estudios Públicos (CEP) in December 2019 had citizens identify the issues that the government should prioritise: pensions (64 per cent), healthcare (46 per cent), education (38 per cent) and wages (27 per cent). On this list of priorities, constitutional reform was in eleventh place with only 7 per cent of the votes (CEP, 2019).

As previously stated, initiating the constituent process required certain pre-existing social and political conditions that must be understood. In this section, I will focus on the first of these conditions: renewed social activism. Then, in the following section, I will analyse the political-institutional factors that led to this process.

The first question that needs to be answered is why people protest in Chile. Between 1983 and 1989, there was an intense cycle of protests against the dictatorship, led by social organisations and political parties opposed to the military regime. Looking at how protests are remembered in history takes us back to worker and class movements at the end of the nineteenth and beginning of the twentieth centuries. This also includes feminist struggles during almost all of the twentieth century, as well as the resistance movements of native people, particularly the Mapuche people who had historically resisted the occupation of their territory in Southern Chile. However, once democracy returned in 1990, social organisations suffered an important decline, at least until 2006 when middle-school students reprised their leading role in protests. Effectively, since 2006 and up until the present day, a new cycle of activism has emerged, in which different actors have brought up their demands using different kinds of protest. Native, environmental, student, regionalist and feminist movements – as well as those of other social actors – have demanded improvements to their quality of life and have taken to the streets to protest.

What explains this new cycle of protests? Literature has come up with three explanations. The first is related to social inequality. As the country developed economically in the 1990s, the distribution of the rewards of this growth was very unequal. As this injustice became more and more obvious, social organisations began to demand their right to a quality education, better pensions, better access to healthcare and better wages. The protests that were organised can be interpreted as rebelling against an unfair system – the so-called 'neoliberal model' (Ruiz Encina, 2019).

A second explanation is that the capitalist modernisation process itself explains social discontent. During the 1990s, a new middle class emerged with access to education, healthcare, loans and better job opportunities. This new middle class also had access to better material conditions, which led them to demand a better quality of life. For example, for the first time in history, large groups of students had access to university education, but this put their families into greater debt. Social demands, from this perspective, cannot be understood as objections against an unjust system but rather must be associated with demands for greater inclusion into the capitalist system (Peña, 2020).

Complementing the other arguments, a third one indicates that, since the return to democracy, there has been a disconnect or maladjustment between the party system and society. The centre-left Concertación coalition that managed to control the Executive between 1990 and 2010 focused its political attention on access to state power. As a result of this effort, it neglected territorial links with society's lower and middle classes. Political parties focused their political actions on managing the state and not on strengthening their links with social organisations at a local level, therefore producing an 'elitisation' of politics. This allowed right-wing parties to establish renewed territorial links with society's lower classes. Over a period of ten years, the electoral decline of centre parties and, in particular, of the Christian Democratic party (PDC) became visible, as well as an important increase in the number of votes for the right-wing party Independent Democratic Union (UDI) (Garretón, 2016).

The previous explanations do not appear to be mutually incompatible. There is no doubt that the economic and social modernisation process encouraged the emergence of new demands. However, at the same time, this process occurred mainly at the cost of individuals going into debt. Between 2000 and 2018, the debts of families significantly increased, as they came to depend more and more on their own credit cards to access education, healthcare and consumer goods. In this way, it can be said that this modernisation mainly depended on individual debt and, to a lesser extent, on the state itself.

The protest dynamic, then, should be understood both as a demand for inclusion and as an objection to economic and social injustices. The (secondary school and university) student movement was one of the first to reinvent itself after the return to democracy. To do so, it brought to the fore the demand for quality education in order to put an end to the existing gaps between private fee-paying and public education. It also began to demand free education, given the high levels of individual debt caused by going to university. From 2016 onwards, a movement called 'No more AFP' emerged, demanding that pensions be improved, as well as a change to the pension system itself. In Chile, the pension system depends on individual contributions from workers and is administered by private companies (called AFPs). At the same time, these demands were joined by others – for example, environmental ones – that emerged to object to companies whose activities seriously affected the quality of life of people living in certain parts of the country. The indigenous movement also emerged, demanding the recuperation of land and the recognition of native people. The feminist movement should also be mentioned, since it launched an important campaign to legalise abortion in 2015–2016 (Donoso and Von Bülow, 2017).

The protest dynamic over the last decade (2011–2021) has two main characteristics. Firstly, it involves social groups whose protests are not necessarily coordinated. Each group had its own agenda and range of action, which is why there have been high levels of fragmentation. Only at the end of the decade, in August 2019, was a 'Social Unity Roundtable' set up of 150 social and union organisations to draw up an agenda of social demands for Piñera's government. Among others, the main workers' organisation (CUT), the Union of Teachers, the March 8th Feminist Group (8M), the Confederation of University Students, the 'No More AFP' movement and the Civil Servant Association took part.

The second characteristic refers to the distancing of these movements from traditional political parties. During the dictatorship, the majority of social organisation leaders had a clear party leaning associated with the main centre-left, something that is now much less clear. Left-wing parties continue to predominate in the main social organisations, such as the Communist Party (in the CUT) and the Humanist party (in the Union of Teachers), while leaders from a new left-wing alliance called the Frente Amplio have appeared in other organisations. However, many other organisations made explicit reference to how they had distanced themselves from traditional political parties. The 'Social Unity Roundtable' – at least in reflective terms – emerged as a place to challenge the political elite and force them to respond to social and territorial demands.

The last characteristic refers to social activism's progressive 'constitutionalisation', to the extent that the proposed reforms hit a brick wall with the Constitution. Several of the social actors' demands involved a substantial revision of either specific articles of the Constitution or of the regulations found in the Constitutional Organic Law. Any legal changes to these needed a special quorum of four-sevenths in Congress to be approved and were therefore considered 'almost-constitutional'. By setting their sights on reforms to the Constitution, many legislative conflicts ended up being settled by the Constitutional Tribunal. This autonomous institution has, over the last decade, taken on a leading role in political and social conflicts. Since it is the more conservative political forces who are dominant in this tribunal, social groups have gained awareness of the relevance of the legal-constitutional structural framework to moving their demands forward.

For example, university students' demands for free, public and quality education involved modifying what was called the Higher Education Constitutional Organic Law, since this law establishes the basis on which the Chilean university system is organised. In the case of access to healthcare, education and pensions, the Constitution gives people the option of choosing between public or private services, limiting the state's options for developing public policies in these sectors. The demand concerning water rights is based on an article in the Constitution that protects the water rights of private owners. This makes Chile the only country in the world where private individuals' right to water is protected by the state. This has led to territorial protests aimed at abolishing this article.

Other demands are associated with the absence of a constitutional framework for certain rights. For example, organisations for the homeless have demanded the incorporation of decent housing as a fundamental right. The indigenous movement has demanded incorporating both the notion of a state consisting of several nationalities into the Constitution and a series of political self-determination rights, as well as territorial, cultural and jurisdictional ones.

In 2013, a 'Mark your Vote' movement emerged, calling on people to mark their ballot paper with a 'CA' in the presidential elections to request a Constituent Assembly. The movement captured the interest of the media and of certain actors in society, who used this campaign to base their protests on. According to an unofficial count, at least 10 per cent of the votes were marked. Between 2014 and 2018, the government developed a constituent process that encouraged debate on a new Constitution and different social movements were able to see how their demands were more or less directly related with how the Constitution was designed. The fact that this was also a Constitution that was originally drawn up and imposed during a dictatorship meant society was in favour of it being replaced.

Two social activism events marked the protests' 'constitutionalisation'. In 2016, during the second government of socialist Michelle Bachelet (2014–2018), the government pushed through a reform to allow union ownership – in other words, in companies, to allow negotiations to only be carried out with trade unions and not with groups of worker negotiators. In addition, it proposed that only trade unions could extend the benefits of a group contract to other workers, not the employer. In 2016, the Constitutional Tribunal rejected these two moves, which would have boosted the negotiating power of trade unions, indicating that these measures were unconstitutional. This caused a lot of discontent among union organisations, who regarded the Constitution as an impediment to improving their rights.

Another emblematic case involved abortion. Congress had been debating a bill to legalise abortion since 2015 in three different situations (when the foetus is unviable, when the mother's life is in danger and when the pregnancy is the result of rape). This caused huge political and social controversy and led to a series of protests both by the conservatives who rejected this proposal and by the organisations that supported it. The legislative process lasted two years and, in August 2017, the project was submitted to the Constitutional Tribunal for review. The protests became more intense and more than a hundred organisations made their views known in a scenario that had never be seen before in the country. Finally, the decision was made to accept the project, although it allowed doctors to conscientiously object to carrying out abortions. In any case, the decision caused great debate about the Constitutional Tribunal's role in approving and rejecting bills.

This is how many social demands gained a constitutional element, as a result of the legal barriers in place that prevented promoting certain rights, such as sexual and reproductive rights, employment rights, water rights and the right to access a quality education. This also occurred because of the absence of constitutional provisions to protect and guarantee certain rights, such as the right to housing, the rights of native people and the rights of children.

Factors endogenous to the political system

On its own, the increases in 'constitutionalisation' and in the number of protests do not explain how the constitutional process came about. For thirty years, political forces had avoided constitutional change, with the Constitution setting out a distribution of power that favoured the status quo. This is why protests do not automatically turn into significant constitutional change. In my opinion, certain conditions endogenous to the political system help explain the political-social dynamic in Chile that led first to a social uprising and then to the constituent process. In this section, I will refer to three specific topics: the institutional transformations that significantly revitalised social activism; the government policies that encouraged the constituent debate and the action of epistemic communities that led to political alternatives for constitutional change.

One of the most relevant changes to the cycle being analysed refers to certain institutional changes that unintentionally had an effect on the social sphere. At the beginning of the 2000s, legal changes gave the government greater control over large companies and, in particular, over the Free Competition Tribunal. Between 2006 and 2020, more than 20 cases of collusion were detected in sectors as diverse as pharmacies, chicken farming, toilet paper, supermarkets and medical professional associations (Fuentes, 2019). This kind of institutional change favoured regulating highly concentrated markets but, at the same time, large companies' price-fixing of essential goods caused great upset among the people. In little more than decade, people's trust of public and private institutions disappeared.

This matter is crucial, since several of these cases escalated people's frustration and feelings of anger. One of the most emblematic cases involved toilet paper. In 2015, the National Financial Public Prosecutor's Office accused Chilean company CMPC and a Swedish company of colluding to fix the price of toilet paper to defraud consumers over a ten-year period. Later, a 2016 investigation discovered that there had been collusion between CMPC and the multinational company Kimberly Clark in the nappy market for over almost eight years. The investigation into the first case lasted five years, after which the courts made the companies pay fines and reparations to consumers. In addition, the company and the Chilean state agreed to reimburse consumers, paying everyone who registered to receive this compensation US$ 9. Thirteen million people received compensation, totalling slightly over US$ 117 million. In all, people's perception of large companies abusing their power grew and grew as these types of scandal came to light.

Another relevant institutional reform should also be mentioned. In 2003, for the first time in Chile's history, a law was passed to regulate political campaign financing. This established a way for companies to donate to political campaigns, capped donations and created a system to control electoral spending. Although these reforms were considered a step in the right direction at the time, just over a decade later, the law began to investigate illegal activities involving business groups and politicians. The absence of a way to control this law and the lack of associated sanctions was a huge incentive to receive campaign donations illegally. In addition, the law investigated the undue influence of companies in the discussion of bills that favoured them. These illegalities contributed to the perception of political parties and businessmen abusing their power even more.

Social unease, therefore, was the result of the consecutive, accumulated strain caused by growing levels of individual debt, discontent with the abuses carried out by large companies and distrust in the political elite. The social uprising in Chile should be understood as a complex configuration of material social demands combined with growing discontent with the political and economic elites in positions of power.

The second political-institutional factor is related to societal learning since 2014. Bachelet's second government promised to establish a 'democratic, institutional and participative' constituent process as part of its programme. However, she did not have the political support in Congress for a new Constitution and did not get the 67 per cent of the votes she needed. Nevertheless, President Bachelet decided to embark on a process of citizen dialogue to establish a new Constitution, with the aim of creating the social conditions required for change.

While the majority of right-wing parties refused to be involved with this initiative, the government invited people to come together and talk among themselves and propose constitutional changes. These citizen town halls involved just over 200,000 people. Later, an indigenous constituent process brought together more than 10,000 people. Towards the end of 2017, these proposals were organised and, at the beginning of 2018, when she was about to end her term as president, Bachelet dispatched a bill to totally reform the Constitution, taking into consideration several of the ideas from these town halls (OECD, 2017).

There were significant differences of opinion about how to move forward with the constitutional issue, even among the government parties of the centre-left coalition. The more moderate government coalition ministers did not accept the idea of convening a constituent assembly, instead preferring that Congress itself drew up the new Constitution. For their part, the Socialist party, the Radical party, the Party for Democracy and the Communist party wanted to either hold a referendum or establish a constitutional reform using the constituent assembly to replace the current Constitution (Fuentes and Joignant, 2015).

In summary, Bachelet's constituent process did not lead to a new Constitution. Right-wing parties refused to get involved in the citizen dialogues organised by the government and did not accept the legal reform proposals to establish a new Constitution. The process in itself did, however, act as an important learning process for the people. When the social uprising occurred in October 2019, the people's first reaction was to organise self-convened open citizen meetings at a territorial and neighbourhood level.

For almost two months, social activism got stronger, without any political party intervention playing a relevant role (Fuentes, 2021).

Up until now, we have identified the social and political-institutional conditions that favoured the social uprising and the subsequent constituent process. These social demands were fragmented, although many of them found a common thread in the Constitution and became more cohesive over time. After 2014, the debate on constitutional change was adopted by the elite, although there was still strong resistance from an important segment of parties, particularly the right.

Another element that should be added to the dynamic described refers to an intellectual elite that became gradually more involved in the debate, coming up with ideas, making suggestions and becoming more active in the pursuit of constitutional change. Effectively, in the case of Chile, there is a structured intellectual elite that has actively participated in the political and constitutional debate and has been directly linked to political parties, has created specific constitutional content and has made suggestions and actively taken part in decision making on these matters.

In a previous study (Fuentes, 2021), I reviewed the profile of those who make up this intellectual elite and observed that it incorporates people with a high level of education obtained both in Chile and abroad. Male lawyers from the Metropolitan Region who studied at the University of Chile or the Catholic University of Chile predominate. However, over the last few years, new universities such as the Diego Portales University, the University of Valparaíso, the Austral University and the University of Talca have emerged among this elite, as well as the creation of a network of female constitutionalist lawyers who have started to have a greater presence in the political debate.

What is interesting about this process is the political links established between different parties, clearly involving these intellectuals. We can see the active participation of 'expert' constitutional lawyers in defining the different coalitions' government programmes. They have played a role in coming up with constitutional reform proposals and when decisions are made. For example, when Bachelet's government (2014–2018) established the citizen dialogue process, a Constituent Process Observers' Council was set up. This included constitutionalist female lawyers linked to the main government and opposition parties. Afterwards, when an agreement was reached to replace the Constitution in November 2019, a technical committee was created, including experts such as lawyers and political scientists with different political beliefs. Finally, when elections were held for the constituent convention, some of these lawyers also stood as candidates.

The existence of a critical mass of individuals is highly relevant when it comes to understanding the process that led to proposing a new Constitution.

These are the people who have been coming up with alternatives, drawing up policy options and even making certain political agreements viable so that the Constitution can be replaced. Therefore, just as radicalisation and the intensity of the protests help explain the constituent process, we should also pay attention to the political-institutional conditions that triggered it and to the agents who turned ideas into action.

In the case of Chile, protests have become gradually more intense since at least 2006. The generation of political proposals and actions that put the topic of constitutional change on the agenda and the activation of an intellectual elite that played an active role in the constituent debates have created alternatives to bring about this change. The perfect storm erupted on November 15th 2019 and it is this that I will analyse next.

The political agreement that was part of the constituent process

On November 15th, a little less than a month after the beginning of the uprising, the main political forces in Congress agreed on a way to replace the constitutional text. This was a political response to – partly – contain the postponed social demands. The Communist party excluded itself from this agreement as it criticised the absence of organised social actors – such as union federations, professional associations and trade unions – at the negotiating table.

In a society in which there was already a high level of tension and whose president was weakened, certain right-wing political leaders held informal meetings with sectors of the left-wing opposition. These informal conversations led to an opportunity to change the Constitution. The right-wing parties that were willing to take this step (National Renovation and Evopoli) represented a line of politics that saw the need to provide a convincing response to the social crisis that had emerged. It is worth noticing that the government and the president did not play a leading role in this agreement but were simply spectators to what would be the main agreement of the post-transition period.

On November 15th, a group of parliamentarians and party leaders held a day-long meeting to set out the basic principles of this agreement. A technical committee was also set up to define the text of the constitutional reform that would make the constituent process possible. The constituent process would have to go through Congress and would institutionalise an unprecedented process in Chile's republican history. It would be the first time that the people had been called upon to decide whether they wanted a new Constitution and it would be the first time that the people could elect a convention to write it.

The Covid-19 pandemic meant the electoral calendar had to be changed but, in summary, the constituent process involved four different stages:

(1) An initial referendum (held on October 25th) in which the people were asked whether they wanted a new Constitution and, on a second ballot sheet, who should write it (a mixed convention including parliamentarians or an elected one). Around 80 per cent of the voters approved a new constitution and 80 per cent of these chose a convention elected entirely by citizens.
(2) Afterwards came a second election to choose those who would make up the convention, held on May 15th and 16th 2021. Representatives were elected in the same way as MPs to the Parliament (a proportional system open to all).
(3) The third stage involves the work of the convention, which will last between nine and twelve months (until June 2022), and that started on July 4th 2021.
(4) Finally, a referendum will be held for the people to ratify the text produced by the convention (August 2022).

Described like this, Chile will experience a great deal of electoral activity over the next two and a half years. As well as the three electoral events described (the initial referendum, the election of the convention and the exit referendum), local and regional governor elections (in May 2021) and presidential, regional councillors and congressional elections (November 2011) will also be held. In less than three years, the people will go to the polls at least four times – without taking into consideration second rounds or primaries – to make decisions in ten different areas.

The first milestone was the referendum in October 2020 and there was a high level of uncertainty about how many people would actually vote. The Covid-19 pandemic battered Chile between March and August 2020, making it impossible to predict the turnout. This was important because, if less than 50 per cent of the population voted, the process's legitimacy would be called into question. The day ended up being exemplary, with no violent incidents and 51 per cent of the eligible population voting. Electoral data show that there was a high level of participation in the large urban areas in Central Chile.

From a political point of view, the constituent process divided the political right, since one segment called on rejecting the idea of changing the Constitution while the political forces that negotiated the agreement advocated approving this idea. Therefore, the 80 per cent approval rate cannot be interpreted only as a centre-left triumph. In society, the idea of changing the Constitution gained momentum because it managed to align itself with certain critical aspects of the recent social conflict. What kind of role should the state play in society? Should Chile be a plurinational state that recognises native people? How much autonomy should regions have? What kind of social rights should be established in the Constitution? What role does the state play in healthcare? How are states of emergency regulated?

The 'constitutionalisation' of politics managed to channel social aspirations and it is probably this that was expressed by the 80 per cent: the hope that a new way of coexisting would allow for some of the population's fragile aspirations to be met in a society that recognises diversity, safeguards social rights and possesses a welfare state.

As usually occurs in this type of process, one of the main topics of political discussion has been on how the convention is made up. As has already been mentioned, the originally approved constitutional reform indicated that the convention's members would be chosen using a proportional system open to all that replicated the Parliament's district system. Civil society organisations realised that would imply that only traditional political parties could have any level of representation. Under this system, those who obtained the highest number of votes on the most voted for lists would win. Therefore, individual independent candidates would have to compete against party lists or pacts, which would put them at a huge disadvantage. In a social context marked by anti-partisanship, civil society aspired to a convention that mirrored society rather than reflected the traditional political elite.

During 2020, Congress approved regulations that resolved the original predicament. Firstly, the rule on voting for the convention was changed, establishing the principle of male/female parity both among candidates and in the results. In other words, the lists would be organised so that a woman appeared first, then a man and so on (a zipper system). In addition, once the election was verified, a certain level of correction would be applied to avoid gender over-representation in any one district. For the first time in the worldwide history of constituent assemblies, a parity regulation would be applied. This was made possible thanks to the feminist movement's protests, the ability of experts to have an impact on the legislative debate and their influence on the legislative process the previous year, all of which helped gain majority support for modifying the constituent agreement, although this was not unanimous.

The second reform meant that lists of independent candidates could be drawn up to compete on the same footing as those from political parties. These candidates needed to have a minimum number of supporters and a programme coherent to the list they appeared on. They did not manage to change other key aspects, such as the financing of electoral campaigns and only a partial reform was introduced to give these candidates access to televised electoral slots. The practical result of this reform was a high number of lists – both of political parties and of independent candidates grouped together – for the elections in May 2021.

The third reform, also approved by Congress, reserved 17 seats for indigenous people. The ten native populations recognised by the Chilean state would have at least one representative in the convention, with the Aymara people having two and the Mapuche people seven. Indigenous voters would use special ballot paper and have the opportunity to vote for these reserved seats or candidates from their district. This was unprecedented in the country's history, since Chile has never before incorporated recognition of native people at a constitutional level and there is, in fact, a lingering conflict between the Chilean state and the Mapuche people.

In the debate about the convention's composition, a proposal was also made to incorporate candidates with disabilities (5 per cent), which was approved, as well as one seat in the convention for people of African descent, which was eventually rejected.

Therefore, although this convention ended up being similar to the current Parliament from a political point of view (with 155 seats), the regulations that were approved allowed for parity. The convention established through the May 2021 elections includes 77 women and 78 men, with native people making up 11 per cent through the reserved seats system and, in an unprecedented situation, independents making up 30 per cent. From a political distribution point of view, 24 per cent of the convention is right-wing, 23 per cent moderate centre-left wing and a little more than 40 per cent left-wing. The ideological positions of the remaining 13 per cent are still unknown, but the majority are probably centre-left.

From an electoral point of view, what is novel about this conformation is the defeat of the right-wing coalition, which aspired to win at least a third of the convention to therefore be able to exercise some kind of veto. The appearance of lists of independent candidates with an important history of social activism, who do not belong to traditional political parties and are highly involved in social causes linked to the environment, feminism, the defence of human rights and grass-roots social organisations is also noteworthy. From a socio-demographic point of view, the convention will be dominated by people with a university education (88 per cent), of whom 44 per cent are lawyers and 12 per cent teachers. The majority of the convention's members (68 per cent) do not belong to a political party, although several of them appeared on party lists.

A key aspect that has been one of the main issues in the comparative experience refers to the decision-making rule. The political agreement established that the convention should be governed by a quorum of two-thirds, both internally and for any regulation it approves. The latter implies that anything that leads to consensus will be ratified in the new Constitution. Since no political or social force has a substantial majority, the foreseeable result is of negotiation and agreement between majorities.

What effects can we hope for from this constituent process? Firstly, as one in a scenario with a high level of unrest, we should not expect the waters of social anxiety to calm down in the next few months. In fact, quite to the contrary, the referendum and the following stages of the constituent process will lead to important social and political controversy surrounding the founding principles of the Republic. A lot will depend on the ability of those drawing up this Constitution to channel demands, make debates viable and hold substantial discussions about the state, market, social rights, the recognition of native people and a long list of other topics.

This process will therefore be an institutionalised one, with the rules of the game defined in the constitutional text. Since the political agreement has turned into a constitutional one, the actors involved must travel down the recently described roadmap. Given the balance of power of the previously mentioned forces, the convention's work will involve a sophisticated exercise of hashing out agreements to guarantee certain minimum common denominators, stretching from the country's right to its left.

Finally, the political agreement included certain other items limiting the convention. There was an attempt to limit the uncertainty surrounding the multiple interests at play for the same economic and political actors that propelled this process forward. For example, the convention has a year to carry out its work. After this year, it will be dissolved, whether or not it has managed to agree on a constitutional text. In addition, if the people reject the text proposed by the convention in the exit referendum, the current Constitution will remain in place. These two issues mean that there is a powerful incentive to reach an agreement.

An additional issue involves the convention's procedural aspects. If these are affected – for example, if a group of convention members decide to change the quorum for approval – a quarter of the members can ask the Supreme Court, which can only make decisions about procedural issues and never about content, to revise this change.

Could the convention (the constituent power) alter the predefined rules of the game of Congress (the constituted power)? In theory, the convention could change these conditions although, politically, it is highly unlikely that this will occur. In a highly fragmented political scenario, it is unthinkable that a single political way of thinking could monopolise the political arena. For this reason, practically every political force – including the Communist party that did not originally approve of this agreement – is playing according to the rules of the game described here.

This is why the role that organised civil society plays – in terms of its impact on the convention – will be key over the coming year. We have already seen the effectiveness of the feminist movement in incorporating parity into the convention. The indigenous movement has also had a degree of success. It is highly likely that civil society organisations emerge voicing their demands based on the debates associated with social and employment rights, the recognition of native people, water rights, natural resources, the protection of biodiversity and the right to life, among many other topics.

From a content point of view, we will very likely see more intense and broader debates about the State's role in protecting economic, social and cultural rights; the change of the political regime with a view to mitigating the exacerbated presidentialism of the Chilean system; the introduction of direct democracy mechanisms, currently inexistent in the country; limiting the Constitutional Tribunal's attributes; recognising native people and regulating and protecting environmental matters and the previously mentioned common public goods.

The institutionalisation of the constituent process in Chile, accepted today by all the political forces and also by businesses, has undoubtedly turned into an opportunity to at least alter a model that has favoured the market above the state and individualism above cooperation. Like any opportunity, however, it can be used or wasted by those with the task of writing a new pact for political and social coexistence. This is what remains to be seen.

Conclusion

In this chapter, I have argued that the social uprising and the political dynamic of replacing the Constitution have a middle-term explanation: certain structural changes to society have increased society's expectations of inclusion, but at the same time have triggered frustration and anger. This scheme of accelerated modernisation mainly depends on individuals' ability to go into debt. In the same way as opportunities were created to get an education or buy a house or certain goods, people's personal debt has also increased significantly. There is also a highly concentrated economic structure in which, over time, cases of collusion and abuses of power have come to light and upset the people. It is not only inequality itself that leads to protests, but also perceived abuses of power and injustice.

From a political-institutional point of view, there has also been a double-sided progression. On one hand, certain institutional reforms have made abuses of power more evident. In this case, there are two examples: policies to control free competition and reforms on how politics is financed. On the other hand, there is also a political dynamic that invoked constitutional change as a requirement for improving the conditions of democratic coexistence.

The storm came to a head on October 18th 2019, when a group of students jumped over the barriers on the underground, protesting about a hike in public transport prices. This apparently minor incident gave way to an intense cycle of protests that, among other things, led to an agreement on replacing the Constitution being reached.

This description suggests that, to understand the political dynamic of these circumstances, attention must be paid to the longer-term trends being developed in society. We can see that politics has become progressively more 'constitutionalised', as different political and social actors come to identify the Constitution as an impediment to social and political changes, something that does not protect certain rights and as a barrier that prevents majorities from expressing themselves. This poses an important question about the way in which these expectations are related to the future socio-political reality, since we know a constitutional text or regulation will not solve every problem a society faces.

In Chile, a new Constitution will not automatically or magically solve inequality, injustice, gender inequality and an inequality in the access to power. A Constitution creates a general framework through which to distribute power, rights and responsibilities in a society, but it depends on the agency of those involved to turn this into policies that resolve wide-ranging differences. That is why one of the concerns surrounding the constituent process currently taking place involves the ability of politicians and key figures in society to clarify and control people's expectations and create the conditions needed to resolve and channel social conflicts.

All in all, the institutional conditions behind the constituent process reflect the middle-term trends described in this chapter, due to the fact that it is a highly institutionalised process. At the end of the day, to a great extent, everything will depend on the agreements that the main political parties and emerging social forces incorporated into the convention managed to reach. In addition, reflecting new social trends, noteworthy innovations have been incorporated such as parity and seats reserved for native people. Therefore, the institutional measures adopted clearly reflect the socio-political dynamic of a country that is advancing towards shaping a new social pact of coexistence.

Note

1 This essay is part of a research project (N° 1170025) on the constituent process in Chile, financed by the Chilean National Fund for Scientific and Technological Development (FONDECYT). Some of the arguments expressed here appear in the author's book *La Transición Inacabada: El proceso politico chileno 1990–2020* (Santiago: Catalonia, 2021).

References

CEP (2019) *Estudio Nacional de Opinión Pública N° 84*. Santiago: Centro de Estudios Públicos.
Donoso, S. and M. von Bülow (eds.) (2017) *Social Movements in Chile: Organization, Trajectories and Political Consequences*. New York: Palgrave Macmillan.
Fuentes, C. (2019) *La Erosión de la democracia*. Santiago: Catalonia.
Fuentes, C. (2021) *La Transición Inacabada: El proceso político chileno 1990–2020*. Santiago: Catalonia.
Fuentes, C. and A. Joignant (eds.) (2015) *La Solución Constitucional*. Santiago: Catalonia.
Garretón, M.A. (ed.) (2016) *La gran ruptura: Institucionalidad política y actores sociales en el Chile del siglo XXI*. Santiago: LOM.
Levitsky, S. and D. Ziblatt (2018) *How Democracies Die*. New York: Baror International.
OECD (2017) *Chile: La participación ciudadana en el proceso constituyente*. Paris: OECD.
Peña, C. (2020) *Pensar el malestar*. Santiago: Tauros.
Pierson, P. (2004) *Politics in Time: History, Institutions, and Social Analysis*. Princeton: Princeton University Press.
Ruiz Encina, C. (2019) *La política en el neoliberalismo: Experiencias latinoamericanas*. Santiago: LOM.

Beyond the revolt
The Chile that is coming

Carlos Peña and Patricio Silva

The name of this epilogue is ironic in that it quite closely reflects what occurred in a part of the intellectual field concerning the events to which this book refers. 'The Chile that is coming' (el Chile que viene) was the name given to a series of seminars at Harvard University at the beginning of the 1990s, in which a generation of Chilean intellectuals came together to examine the path the country would follow in its new modernisation phase. They predicted a successful modernisation in Chile and asked themselves what should be done at an institutional and cultural level to ensure this. The idea was to prevent Chile from falling into the well-known 'middle income trap', as had occurred so many times before in other parts of the world. In these seminars, it was established that Chile desperately needed to modernise its transport system, improve education, redesign both its electoral system and political regime and carry out a series of institutional changes. Although it was insinuated that these could cause setbacks to the country, it never even occurred to them that Chile would find itself in a situation like that of the last few years. It is still worth answering the question, though, about where Chile is headed. The answer, however, should consider the shadow of discontent that currently clouds modernisation, a process that had been referred to during those seminars in an openly celebratory way.

Therefore, it is worth looking back at some of the circumstances that have led to this discontent and which have been explored in the chapters of this book.

On October 18th 2019, Chile was plunged into its worst political, economic and institutional crisis since the fall of the Unidad Popular government in 1973. On that day, a widespread social insurrection occurred that, at first glance, seemed to lack structure and had very heterogenous demands. Although the official reason for the wave of protests was the increase in the price of underground tickets, it soon became clear that this was just a catalyst for a set of different types of demands: some of them cultural, some of them generational and others more similar to class demands. The

DOI: 10.4324/9781003254355-7

majority of these pursued aims that were markedly groundbreaking regarding the economic, political and social systems that had been dominant in Chile since 1990.

Some political analysts, talking about the October 2019 social uprising, later declared that this outburst had been on the cards for a long time. However, the truth is that the October uprising took the majority of Chileans, including the political class, completely by surprise. It is true that secondary school pupils became politically mobilised since 2006. Their demonstrations questioned the educational system and different aspects of what has been called the 'neoliberal model'. These protests against the country's current socioeconomic and political system were reinforced from 2011 onwards by the emergence of a widespread and powerful university student movement, which adopted a quite radical stance. In addition, there were also other visible expressions of social protest from 2011 onwards by different social movements, including environmental groups, Mapuche organisations, sexual minorities and feminists.

However, despite all these examples rejecting the status quo and illustrating the discontent with modernisation, there were also many signs that the majority of Chileans had been generally satisfied with both their lives and the country's economic and social progress since the return to democracy in 1990. There were certainly objective reasons to evaluate the path the country had followed before 2019 in positive terms. From 1990 onwards, Chile was undeniably the most prosperous nation in Latin America. Politically, the country had a successful transition to democracy which, despite being regarded with scepticism in hindsight, occurred both peacefully and with high levels of institutional stability. Economically, Chile became a regional power, with high levels of economic growth and foreign investment and a big international reputation. Socially, Chile achieved a dramatic reduction in its level of poverty, with this falling from 48 per cent in 1990 to 8 per cent at the time of the social uprising. Even institutionally, the Concertación governments had managed to profoundly reform the 1980 Constitution so it could meet the needs of this new democratic reality.

All these notable transformations in people's material conditions were not, however, accompanied by a narrative bringing them into line with the path the majority of people were on. Instead, material improvements were usually presented as the inevitable result of how social processes were handled technically, as if they were spontaneous and not sustained by a consensus elaborated by political processes depending on the circumstances. This has probably contributed to the fact that these structural changes were unable to adapt themselves completely to people's narratives about their own lives. Therefore, during the majority of the Concertación era (1990–2010), the country went through an important depoliticisation process.

The belief spread that this consensus was spontaneous and hence that no discursive efforts were needed. As a result, although the majority of Chileans saw their families get ahead, few were actually able to incorporate these changes into their life's trajectories. A shared narrative would have given them reasons to defend the socio-political and economic system at the heart of the country's important modernisation process both explicitly and convincingly. Therefore, although some left-wing sectors rationalised the population's discontent – attributing it to the predominance of a technocracy – the Concertación's moderate sectors and even the Chilean right were unable to create a powerful legitimising discourse for Chile's political, economic, social and institutional achievements from 1990 onwards. As a result, the enormous change in the Chilean population's material conditions lacked a narrative making it relevant or that came up with a remedy for its diseases over time. Instead, the country's modernisation was conceived as a historical routine that was able to advance on its own.

In the last decade, the speed of material improvement and the decrease in consumerism, as well as generational and migratory issues, have become visible in a society that was becoming more and more attractive in the region. All of this encouraged a gap between the changes that Chilean society had experienced and the subjectivity of its citizens, who could not relate to these changes, even after overcoming the setbacks. It is likely that these discrepancies between the structural changes themselves and Chileans' actual lives and between society and actual experience have contributed to the social upheaval.

What is new about the scenario that emerged from October 18th 2019 onwards in the country – and which the previous factors could not predict – is that the use of extreme levels of violence in social protests was explicitly legitimised. This broke one of the key agreements of democracy – namely, the illegitimacy of using force to promote one's own interests.

The 'Agreement for Social Peace and the New Constitution' signed on November 15th 2019 by a large group of parliamentarians was an important step towards trying to find a political-constitutional way out of the crisis that occurred after October 18th. This agreement was able to restrain the openly insurrectional impetus that some sectors – taking advantage of the political opportunity – were trying to confer on the ongoing protests occurring in different cities around the country. The extreme left and the most radical social movement groups opposed the November agreement, since they saw it as an attempt to defuse a process that, on their opinion, could lead to revolutionary changes.

This agreement paved the way for the constituent process that is taking place today. This process has been plagued by difficulties, such as the diversity of its members. These go from anti-elite groups to the Communist

Party, a weakened right and social democrat sectors that feel guilty about what has happened. All in all, by reaching this agreement, Chile showed that, despite the difficulties faced, high levels of institutionality still exist in the country. As a result, Chile can still be described as an exception in Latin America.

What can we say about the social process's idiosyncrasies examined in this book and how many of them are common to the rest of the Latin American region? The majority of the analysis on the social uprising has tended to concentrate almost completely on Chilean reality, leaving aside any possible international factors and actors who could have influenced the uprising. On one hand, the possible influence of external factors should not be exaggerated, since this would be akin to making the intellectual error of attributing the imbalance in Chile's social life to a deliberate conspiracy. On the other hand, however, it would also be wrong to completely ignore any external influence or not pay any attention to it in any future analysis of what occurred in Chile.

It should be remembered that, on October 8th 2019, just ten days before the social uprising in Chile, there were widespread violent protests in Ecuador as a result of Lenin Moreno's government adopting a series of measures involving budgetary cutbacks. These protests quickly turned into a national revolt, forcing the president and his ministers to abandon the capital city to seek refuge in Guayaquil to avoid a coup. After receiving unequivocal signs of support from the armed forces and repealing the cutbacks announced, Moreno chose to negotiate directly with the different social organisations that had protested in order to re-establish order in the country. On this occasion, Moreno accused Maduro's Venezuelan regime of being involved in the revolt through the participation of political extremists and by providing all kinds of support to the protesters. What happened in Ecuador was closely followed by the Chilean public, with them able to watch live images and reports of what was taking place in this Andean country.

When the social uprising occurred in Chile, it was also initially suggested that the country was the victim of an international conspiracy led by Caracas and Havana, as well as by organisations connected with the so-called São Paulo Forum, in order to try and destabilise and defeat Sebastián Piñera's government. Since becoming president in 2018, Piñera had been the main opponent of Maduro's regime within Latin America, openly criticising it in international forums. Piñera also gave his resolute support to Venezuelan dissidents, even giving special status to the thousands of Venezuelan refugees arriving in Chile, earning him the scorn of Bolivarian governments in Latin America. In addition, long before Piñera came to power, left-wing governments and movements in Latin America had Chile in their sights, due to the fact that, in their eyes, it represented the region's main bastion of neoliberalism. The fact that it was also the most prosperous nation in Latin America and the one with the best social indicators was always a stumbling block to any anti-neoliberal discourse. In any case, up to now, there is no resounding evidence that other countries have been either directly or indirectly involved in Chile's social uprising. Certain declarations made by Nicolás Maduro himself and his right-hand man, Diosdado Cabello, only hours after the rebellion in Chile suggested though that these events were only a taste of the Bolivarian hurricane that would soon creep up on the country. The General Secretary of the Organisation of American States (OAS), Luis Almagro, also pointed his finger in the direction of Caracas and urged this country not to encourage actions that would cause instability in the region.

Another international factor that stands out to political analysts are the many elements that the important protests in Chile and Colombia over the last few years have in common. These two countries have liberal governments that have embraced the free market economy, encouraged foreign investment and have all kinds of close ties with the United States. In addition, both countries' governments have come out strongly against the increase in Venezuelan involvement in the internal affairs of other Latin American countries. Both countries have also constantly criticised the left-wing governments of Nicaragua, Cuba, Venezuela and Bolivia.

In effect, the recent protests in Colombia have been very similar to those occurring in Chile since October 2019. Firstly, both involved an important number of young people and combined entertaining and almost artistic performances, as well as violent groups facing off in battles with the police. In both countries, the unifying stance adopted by the different political and social forces that took to the streets against their respective governments was an opposition to neoliberalism. Comparative studies will probably emerge soon analysing in greater depth both the similarities and the differences of the political-social outbursts in Chile and Colombia.

All these international factors must, of course, be considered, but should not be overly emphasised. As the chapters of this book show, the Chilean process itself has sufficient local factors to explain the events that began in October and what has happened in their wake.

Can any lessons be learnt by the Latin American region from what has happened in Chile and which this book has attempted to analyse? To answer this question, it is useful to mention that some of the factors that seemed to have triggered the protests in the case of Chile still hold appeal for the rest of the region. We are referring to aims such as decreasing poverty, making education accessible to all and the expansion of middle-class groups accessing consumerism. However, the very country that achieved this over only three decades appears to have succumbed to internal fighting and an almost completely widespread unease. This phenomenon is similar to what happened in São Paulo during Lula da Silva's government and to what occurred during the first six months of 2021 in some of the most modernised parts of Colombia.

There have also been riots in Cuba and Ecuador, although these appear to be due to the health crisis produced by the Covid-19 pandemic. In fact, all these phenomena have – at least partially – coincided with the pandemic. Therefore, the two sources of predictability in life that allow people to escape uncertainty – that is the regularity of both nature and institutions – have been weakened. The chaos of nature has been added to the region's traditional institutional instability. Both of these phenomena have occurred in almost every Latin American country in the last two years and the pandemic seems to have been what has most influenced the protests.

The case of Chile is, however, an exception in this scenario and this is perhaps why it is an interesting case study. The social uprising in Chile, for example, happened months before the pandemic. In addition, Chile has been one of the countries in the region that has best managed to control the pandemic up to now, partly thanks to its greater financial wellbeing and the efficiency of its public policies.

What explains, then, discontent in Chile when, even during a pandemic, its institutions seem to be capable of efficiently carrying out public policies? Why, despite all this, are its citizens still upset? As has been seen, this book has put forward several hypotheses to explain what has occurred. Some of these hypotheses draw attention to the fact that greater wellbeing inevitably changes people's expectations, making them more autonomous and demanding. This is what literature calls 'the welfare paradox', particularly if greater wellbeing emerges from the promise of greater future growth (that feeds people's willingness to go into debt). All this is accompanied by an enormous expansion in access to education, allowing historically excluded sectors to become professionals (when they regarded them from afar, these degrees seemed akin to a noble title). Therefore, this is when any setbacks to expanding wellbeing and consumerism can result in overwhelming frustration.

For this very reason, one of the chapters of this book describes the existence of a disillusioned generation. Another chapter draws attention to an improved wellbeing that is, however, perceived by the people as a house of cards that could come tumbling down at the slightest movement or due to crisis or illness. Another contribution suggests that all these processes make up the disease of modernisation and are effects of a growth that has been disregarded due to the inability of those who inspired it to understand their own success. All these factors have provided a political opportunity for forces with a reason to oppose the modernising process. It is possible to predict that these same factors will be replicated in countries that will manage to radically change their material conditions of existence, without dealing with the imbalances this causes, and that we have analysed in this book.

There is therefore a factor that has probably had an important impact on the Latin American region, beyond the so-called sociological components already mentioned. This factor is distinctly political.

In the last few decades, Latin America has seen a new left appear that has distanced itself from the old issues that made up its ideological identity in the 1960s. Given its traditional rejection of imperialism, this new left made an effort to become involved in globalisation. Faced with the old class struggle, it has focused on encouraging social mobility and, faced with the traditional rejection of market forces, has begun to view the market as the driving force behind wellbeing. In addition, it has started to value democracy, putting aside the old idea that this was only made up of a handful of merely formal liberties. In short, over the last few decades in the region, a left has appeared that is open to capitalist modernisation. This is the so-called third way left. In the case of Chile in particular – and although the same occurred with Fernando Henrique Cardoso in Brazil – this left has managed to hegemonise the bloc of power to which it belongs and subordinate the sectors that have continued to harbour nostalgia for the old ideologies of the 1960s.

As we have seen, one of the chapters in this book suggests that an important aspect of the phenomenon is made up of this left with its old ideals, which was dormant during the modernisation that occurred in Chile. This left was thought to have been suddenly culturally defeated and then reborn as a result of the political opportunity the crisis provided, launching an attempt to return to its former glory. In other words, this left took advantage of the political opportunity provided by the crisis hinted at – in particular, by the relative failure of the expansion of wellbeing – to develop a strategy openly opposing institutions. To do so, it gathered together a very heterogenous set of demands, many connected to identity, with the aim of aligning them and constructing a new hegemony.

This type of process is almost always accompanied by intellectual assessments to make it plausible. In the case of Latin America, this seems to have emerged from the ideas on radical democracy that Ernesto Laclau promoted and which have a specific kind of appeal. He suggested that contemporary society is a distorted one in which the centre has proliferated and in which the state has lost its pivotal position. In a society with these characteristics, demands abound and have very different features. Laclau calls this fragmented set of demands democratic demands juxtaposed within the political process. Soon however – and this is one of the left's tasks – one of these demands manages to organise all the others from top to bottom, turning them into the demands of the people. At this point, Laclau call this populism, involving an expansion of recognition and wellbeing towards excluded sectors that becomes stable in a new hegemony. Described as such, populism is not a defect but a necessary step towards constituting a new political subject, the people. In this way, the people hegemonise social life until a new exclusion is revealed and the process begins all over again.

These ideas may help us understand part of the phenomenon occurring both in Chile and in other countries in the region, such as Argentina. In both cases, there is a proliferation of all types of demands, which left-wing forces are trying to organise from top to bottom in order to construct a new hegemony.

A look at the Chilean constitutional convention – to whose initial process one of the chapters in this book refers – confirms part of this phenomenon. One of the forces uniting an important number of the convention's members is the so-called 'People's List' (lista del pueblo), which brings together demands of a diverse nature. Some of these relate to class, others are cultural, some are linked to feminist movements and so forth. Together with this, the convention itself is putting the recognition of more diverse identities at the centre of its work. This can be seen by the fact that, a month after it was set up, dozens of flags representing different identities were hung at the entrance of the former Congress where the convention was in session.

These circumstances mean it can be surmised that Chile is in the midst of a process that not only involves reconstructing institutions – through which the constitutional debate is channelled – but also involves demands that are unfolding in a very heterogenous way. A large number of these are the result of the modernisation the country has experienced. It still remains to be seen whether this multiplicity of demands can be incorporated into modernisation or whether they will acquire a different form as a result of a new hegemony.

Despite the many uncertainties for Chile's immediate future, it is highly likely that, irrespective of the final wording of the new Constitution, the Chilean population will not be appeased in the short term, as opposed to prior to October 2019, when this was something that had helped the country achieve the degree of political stability it was known for. This experience indicates that a constitutional text needs time to gain legitimacy. This happened with the 1925 Constitution, which was the predecessor to the 1980 version. This eventually helped guide Chile's development for a large part of the twentieth century, creating what has been called the State of Compromise (1932–1970). The country enjoyed a long period of stability during this time, with new actors gradually incorporated into the political system. This cycle ended at the beginning of the 1970s when the political system's expansion triggered expectations that the economic and productive system were unable to satisfy.

Will the Chile of the future now enter a new cycle taking it towards what is normally called development, a stable democracy and wellbeing that extends to all sectors of society? This will, of course, depend on multiple circumstances that it is impossible to predict. Judging by what has occurred up to now, however, the challenge Chile faces consists of avoiding what could be called the pathologies of modernisation. In addition, the country needs to be capable of providing rules that allow for cooperation within a society that is becoming more and more diverse and pluralist. These rules should encompass at least three challenges. In the first place, they should recognise the multiculturality that, after the extensive predominance of the idea of a consolidated nation from the nineteenth century onwards, has come to light over the last few decades. Secondly, they should shape social rights to guide future policies and correct the divisive effect produced by the class structure. Finally, they should guarantee the civil and political rights typical of a liberal democracy.

Of course, even if it meets these challenges, there is no chance that Chilean society will go back to what it used to be. It is more likely that the modernisation the country has experienced – and the defects that have accompanied it – has changed Chilean society for good. This modernisation has created expectations of material wellbeing, of a distribution of risk and of cultural diversity that the new generations must deal with.

In the seminars held at Harvard University, mentioned at the beginning of this epilogue, enthusiasm for Chile's modernisation abounded. At the same time though, there was an underlying cautiousness regarding the challenges to be faced. The seminars on 'the Chile that is coming' were an effort to explain what was to come. They were also an expression of Chilean society's desire to modernise itself and adopt democratic practices without setbacks. As far as their ability to predict the future was concerned, these seminars, which were held over several years, did not manage to correctly presage everything. Nevertheless, both the aims that fuelled them – the modernising drive and the desire for a healthy democracy – and the conditions needed for these to occur are certainly still present in the country.

Index

activism 32, 87, 88, 90, 91, 92, 94, 98
Allende, Salvador 5, 28, 29, 30, 31, 32, 33, 34, 36, 40, 45n2; *see also* Unidad Popular
anarchism 3
anomie 10, 16, 17, 62, 63, 64, 65, 66
APEC 2, 8
Argentina 110
authoritarian legacy 1, 32, 57
auto-complacientes 38
auto-flagelantes 39, 41, 42
Aylwin, Patricio 34, 37

Bachelet, Michelle 30, 31, 39, 42, 43, 45n2, 45n5, 58, 59, 87, 91, 93, 94
Bolivia 107
Bourdieu, Pierre 14, 53, 54, 63, 64, 65, 66

Catholic Church 16, 17, 21, 22
Che Guevara 32, 33
Christian Democratic Party (PDC) 32, 36, 37, 38, 43, 45n4, 88
civil society 39, 97, 100
collusion 44, 92, 100
Communist Party 3, 30, 37, 38, 42, 43, 95, 99
Concertación coalition 30, 31, 34, 35, 36, 37–44, 45n1, 80, 88, 104, 105
consensus 34, 38, 99, 104, 105
constitutional change 1, 7, 12, 20, 25, 86, 87, 91–95, 100
constitutional convention 6, 23, 24, 25, 44, 67n8, 80, 86, 94, 95–101, 110
Constitution of 1980 2, 5, 6, 7, 30, 34, 37, 40, 73, 85, 104, 110
consumer goods 12, 36, 89

consumerism 8, 9, 13–16, 21, 105, 106, 108
COP25 2, 8
corruption 79
Covid-19 81, 82, 96, 108
Cuba 4, 32, 36, 37, 107, 108
CUT 43, 89

democratic transition 6, 37, 41, 51, 56, 57, 72, 73, 76, 79, 85, 95, 104
democratisation 57, 61
depoliticisation 34, 43, 104
diversity 50, 97, 100, 105, 111

economic growth 1, 3, 38, 45n4, 49, 51, 57, 104
Ecuador 106, 108
emotions 17, 19, 30
experts 60, 71, 94, 97

feminist movement 3, 59, 60, 61, 87, 88, 89, 97, 98, 100, 104, 110
foreign investment 38, 104, 107
framing 39, 42
Frei, Eduardo 32
Frente Amplio 31, 43, 80, 89, 104
frustration 6, 14, 41, 49, 54, 56, 70, 79, 81, 92, 100, 108

generational factor 3, 5, 9, 10, 16, 22, 49, 50, 51, 60, 66
Güell, Pedro 45n5

health care 3, 6, 8, 61, 62, 72, 73, 75–79, 81, 87–90, 97, 108
higher education 2, 5, 7, 8, 42, 48, 49–54, 59, 90, 103, 105
housing 62, 90, 91, 100

Index 113

identity 5, 10, 17, 23, 24, 25, 66, 109
ideology 3, 4, 15, 17, 19, 21, 33, 37, 39, 43, 51, 59, 62, 64, 98, 109
income 6, 8, 48, 50–56, 62, 63, 70, 71, 74–82
indebtedness 6, 7, 55, 56, 58, 71, 76–79, 88, 89, 93, 100, 108
indigenous movement 89, 90, 93, 98, 100
individualism 100
intellectuals 7, 31, 39, 41, 87, 94, 95, 103

job insecurity 76–78, 81; *see also* unemployment

Lechner, Norbert 41
legitimacy 5, 6, 11, 12, 21–23, 32, 71, 73, 74, 79, 80, 81, 82, 96, 105

Maduro, Nicolás 4, 106, 107
Mapuche people 87, 9; *see also* indigenous movement
Marxism 13, 15, 18, 20, 23, 37
Mayol, Alberto 31
memory 20, 24, 25, 30
meritocracy 6, 13, 14, 15, 16, 51, 58
middle class 2, 6, 7, 9, 21, 36, 44, 52, 60, 61, 62, 63, 64, 74, 75, 81, 88, 107, 108
military coup 5, 29, 35, 36
military regime 29, 30, 33, 34, 35, 37, 41, 44, 87
modernisation 1, 4, 5, 7, 8, 9–22, 41, 45, 48, 49, 51, 62, 63, 85, 88, 89, 100, 103–105, 108, 109–111
Moulian, Tomás 41

neoliberalism 2, 4, 5, 19, 29, 31, 38, 42, 45n3, 107
Nicaragua 37, 107
Nueva Mayoría 30, 31, 43, 44, 45n2, 23

OECD 39, 49, 52, 53, 54, 76, 78, 93
Organisation of American States 107

Parliament 5, 6, 32, 34, 35, 38, 72, 95, 96–98, 105
Party for Democracy 93
penguin revolution 45n3, 57, 58, 59, 73
pension system 3, 6, 61, 71, 73, 75–79, 81, 87, 88, 89, 90
Piñera, Sebastián 1–4, 8, 20, 29, 30, 31, 32, 40, 42, 43, 45n1, 69, 70, 71, 86, 89, 106

Pinochet, Augusto 1, 5, 6, 7, 21, 28, 30, 32, 34, 35, 37, 38, 40, 44, 56, 58, 61, 73, 85; *see also* military regime
police 3, 5, 107
política de acuerdos 30, 31, 34
political cleavage 7, 9, 20–21, 23, 28, 29, 32–33, 35–37, 40, 44
political elite 67n8, 81, 90, 93, 97
political stability 1, 2, 8, 34, 38, 39, 43, 45n4, 72, 81, 85, 104, 107, 108, 110
poverty 1, 2, 6, 8, 34, 38, 52, 54, 56, 70, 72, 74, 75, 79, 82, 85, 104, 107
prestige 2, 14, 15, 55
public policies 38, 51, 90, 108

Quintana, Jaime 30, 31

radicalisation 10, 28–35, 44, 95
radical left 30, 35–38, 42, 43, 44
regulations 16, 60, 90, 97, 98, 101
representation 11, 35, 71, 73, 78, 97

slogans 4, 30, 35
social discontent 4, 5, 6, 9–12, 88
social inequality 8, 9, 12, 14, 15, 33, 40, 44, 45n5, 50, 61, 77, 82, 88, 100, 101
socialism 29, 33, 36, 40, 44
social justice 61, 79
social media 32, 55, 61
social mobility 50, 52, 57, 61, 66
social security 6, 62, 71, 81
state of compromise 21, 110
stratification 15, 64
student movement 30, 31, 39, 42, 43, 57–59, 89, 104

technocracy 38, 39, 105

UNDP 9, 41, 45n5, 73
unemployment 33, 82
Unidad Popular 28, 29, 30, 31, 32, 33, 36, 44, 45nn2–4
United States 69, 73, 107
university degree 14, 55, 66

Venezuela 4, 106
violence 3, 9, 35, 44, 59, 60, 105

Weber, Max 15, 20
welfare paradox 5, 12, 13, 14
World Bank 8, 39, 52, 75, 82

For Product Safety Concerns and Information please contact our EU
representative GPSR@taylorandfrancis.com
Taylor & Francis Verlag GmbH, Kaufingerstraße 24, 80331 München, Germany

www.ingramcontent.com/pod-product-compliance
Lightning Source LLC
Chambersburg PA
CBHW052101230426
43662CB00036B/1740